RECLAIMING POWER

Building a Stronger Resistance
in the Age of Trump

Barbara Peterson
Nonviolent Citizens Action

Published by Piscataqua Press
32 Daniel St., Portsmouth, NH 03801
www.piscataquapress.com

ISBN: 9781944393342

Printed in the United States

nonviolentcitizenaction.org

Table of Contents

Introduction

Today's Resistance is not powerful enough to defeat Trump. However, it can be. If we learn the theory, history, and techniques of nonviolent action that have been practiced throughout history and written about most extensively in recent years, we can build a Resistance formidable enough to force Trump and his cohorts to step down. Furthermore, we can create societal structures that effectively oppose Trumpism: an oppressive political, economic, and cultural system that unapologetically places white, Christian, heterosexual, cisgendered men in positions of unjust dominance over all others.

I use the term *the Resistance* (with a capital R) as an umbrella term. It includes hundreds of thousands of different citizen action groups that have formed in the US and around the world to oppose Trump and his policies. From local community groups to large national organizations such as Indivisible and MoveOn, the Resistance is the name for all of these groups that are actively engaged in protesting Trump's destructive influence. Although many Democrats have jumped on board the Resistance, and some Republicans and Independents have also joined, I want to make it clear that I am not specifically talking about any political party. The Resistance is comprised of a broad range of partisan and nonpartisan associations. Groups such as 350.org, the MeToo movement, and the Never Again gun reform activists are examples of non-partisan groups who are part of the Resistance.

In addition, there are thousands of community groups in every state that are non-partisan. They are willing to work with any elected official who supports the goals of the Resistance. While it is true that the vast majority of politicians who have come out in support of Resistance values and objectives are Democrats, we would be wise to be wary of false prophets. It is naïve to think that all Democrats in office and running for office are people of their word. If we realize that some may be merely using the Resistance for their own gains, we will be prepared if needed to pressure them to follow through on their promises and stated views.

This book seeks to show what the Resistance is doing well and what it can be doing better to become far more effective. While the Resistance has made and continues to make impressive gains through mass protests and petitioning the government, we must do far more to entirely topple the authority of Trump and the structures that support him. Generally speaking, the Resistance would be best served if it incorporated the following changes in order to be a serious and realistically effective challenge to Trump's power.

1. Develop a more formal structure that allows the different groups to unite, when necessary, into one massive movement.

2. Form national leadership who help develop a unified set of goals, objectives, and strategic campaigns to guide Resisters into acting as a cohesive whole.

3. Engage in hundreds of different methods, far more than marches and contacting political officials, to successfully dismantle the pillars of support upon which Trump and Trumpism rely for their power.

4. Recognize that permanent structures in society must be built in order for the people to continually ensure power-holders meet the needs of American citizens rather than their own selfish agendas.

In effect, the Resistance needs to become far more organized. It must adopt the strategies and structures inspired by powerful resistance leaders in history such as Gandhi and Martin Luther King, Jr. and written extensively about by scholars in the field of nonviolent action.[1]

PETERSON

While Indivisible started out as a national organization to take down Trump, they only advocate for and instruct their members to engage in a limited set of actions and techniques. Indivisible promotes what I term "political involvement" methods, which are important and bring needed changes. They guide Resisters in putting pressure on government leaders by making phone calls and showing up at legislative hearings to persuade politicians to oppose Trump. As vital as these actions are, they alone are insufficient to defeat Trump and the new extreme political agenda he has inspired.

Trump currently enjoys a Republican majority in both Houses. Although Republicans have been battling each other over proposed laws, with only a couple exceptions, they all support extremist right-wing policies, regardless of how many of their constituents express opposition. Even if there is a Blue Wave in November 2018, we are far from assured that, once in office, our newly elected representatives will do what it takes to restore decency, equality, economic justice, and environmental health. The Resistance must be fully prepared to employ a wide array of nonviolent methods that can successfully hold our leaders to account, regardless of who they are or what party they represent.

The urgency of opposing Trump cannot be overstated. Every day he is having an increasingly disastrous impact on our government and society. He took children away from their parents and put them in cages, alone, terrified, and crying, then his supporters had the gall to justify this using the Christian Bible. He adulates authoritarian dictators and has repeatedly claimed he would like to model himself after them. The GOP tax policy threatens to destroy the middle class, and Trump's tariffs as well as his open hostility to our allies with his uninformed, middle school bullying tactics risk alienating our friends and compromising our economy. And with Justice Kennedy retiring, *Roe v. Wade* is at risk along with other vital legal protections for women and minorities if a conservative is appointed to the Supreme Court. With all of this, in addition to our current administration's war on truth, the US is taking a decisive step closer each day towards right-wing extremism and even, in many cases, fascism. Furthermore, Trump has sparked and emboldened an ever-increasing amount of hate crimes in the US, making Trumpism a significantly dangerous phenomena that will not go away without organized and prolonged opposition, even when Trump himself is no longer President.

In short, our democracy is being threatened. Although voting out Trump and his supporters is certainly a necessary part of the solution, we must do more. Trump has already caused a tremendous amount of harm with his comments and efforts to pass destructive policies. Congress has repealed many of the protections needed to safeguard vulnerable populations as well as the environment. We cannot afford to put all our hopes on an election. There is no guarantee that those who replace our current, self-serving legislators will truly listen to, understand, and take heed of the interests of their constituents, particularly those who suffer most from oppression. Also, counting on elections as a remedy for our current travesties is relying on the same process and system that gave us Trump in the first place.

As scholar and political activist Noam Chomsky stated in an interview with Truthout, even if Democrats win many seats in both Houses in the mid-term elections of November 2018, our problems are far from over.

> [W]hatever gains there might be would not rid us of Trumpism, or its European counterparts. These have grown out of a mixture of authentic grievances and social pathologies – the latter surfacing in part because of the grievances. These are rooted in socioeconomic policies and bitter and so far, quite successful one-sided class struggle. None of this can easily be cast to the dustbin of history.[2]

Since Trump took over as President, the welfare of our democracy, human rights, and environmental health are put increasingly at risk. The problems Trump created and those he exacerbated will not slide quietly back into the shadows even if both houses become led by a Democrat majority. Unless we the people rise up and oppose Trump and Trumpism, we risk having our society erode into an autocracy where financial greed and corruption go virtually unchecked, oppressors become emboldened as they take on leading voices of power, and the wellbeing of our planet is increasingly endangered.

Democratic societies are strongest when they have thriving nongovernmental groups and organizations that help facilitate active and meaningful citizen participation. These groups act to increase the opportunities and civil rights of marginalized persons, protect and enhance the welfare of our planet, and empower all persons to have a voice in shaping the sort of society in which we live. A more organized and structured Resistance creates relationships among different interest groups in society that promote a network of communication and shared goal-making. This is crucial for mutual understandings and the mobilization of collective energies to enact and maintain progressive policies.

Although Trump and the GOP have proven more dangerous than anyone in modern history to the wellbeing of our democracy and its people, they did not come out of nowhere. A major reason for Trump's appeal was that he promised a complete shake-up from business as usual: from a government that increasingly answers to corporate lobbyists rather than their constituents. He offered a unique and tough approach that people hoped would enable him to effectively stand up against politicians who act as if self-serving policies and practices are the norm rather than humble service to the people.

The vast majority of people are angry at the selfish, fraudulent, and deceptive practices that have become the norm in our government over the past several decades. Consider Lyndon Johnson's deception about the Gulf of Tonkin, Nixon's Watergate, Clinton's perjury, George W. Bush's inept handling of 9/11, and Obama's breaking US and international laws with his drone warfare. More recently, in June 2018, all but 10 Democrats supported GOP legislation to increase our military and nuclear spending by $100 billion.

It's difficult to believe that those who claim they want Medicare for all, affordable college education, benefits to the needy, and re-training programs for people in dying industries will truly fight for these things when they vote to put money that could have paid for them into an already excessive and bloated military budget. The point here is not to pick on any particular decision over others. Rather, the point is that our government has proven time and again that it is able and willing to act against the wishes of a vast majority of the people.

The problem, then, is much bigger than Trump, though he is a particularly egregious case of harmful, destructive, greedy, and oppressive corruption in government. The more general problem is that our elected officials, from both sides of the aisle, too often succumb to the Sirens of corporate "gifts," which pulls them away from their duty of attending to the needs of their working class and poor constituents. Populist politicians, therefore, will continue to hold tremendous appeal as long as elected representatives put their own interests above those of the people. Furthermore, although, contrary to his promise, Trump brought "the swamp" to numerous cabinet positions, and he runs Trump Enterprises out of the White House, including selling golf tees with the presidential seal,[3] his appeal will remain strong among Republicans who want to pass harmful tax legislation, among white supremacists and misogynists who enjoy their newly empowered voice, and among his devoted and loyal fans.

Once empowered, people don't simply give up and go away. White supremacists have come out of their hiding places and are enjoying a new sense of power and support from not only the government, but from some very prominent people, such as Sean Hannity of Fox News and the Koch brothers whose billions of dollars carry tremendous influence. Thus, while Trump's power may be significantly weakened if Democrats win the majority in the mid-term elections, the Trump-effect will remain alive and influential, threatening to rise again in different forms and in varying degrees. The increase in racist, sexist, homophobic, and religious intolerance will not simply fade away. Those who believe in equity and justice for all must be prepared for a long-term struggle, and this book will help do that.

One of the reasons we resist, therefore, is to put an end to a system in which narcissistic demagogues like Trump can run virtually unchecked in their selfish pursuit of power. We need to replace it with a more inclusive and participatory system. Today's Resistance can help create such a system through an organized strategic nonviolent movement that alters how our government functions. By engaging in the sort of movement I advocate in this work, we can help re-establish organizations that fight against hate groups, organizations such as those that were dismantled due to millions of dollars cut by the Trump administration.[4] The Resistance can create long-term bonds, cultural and political identifications, relationships among different groups, and social structures in the places where people live every day.

Nonviolent action addresses threats to our nation's people and environment at both the governmental and societal levels. It is therefore not just an answer to Trump and the GOP; it is a way of empowering the people so they play a meaningful role in the decisional processes in our democracy. This book seeks to show how current harmful legislation can be overturned, how the people can put an end to the strengthening voices of authoritarianism, and how the people can restructure power relations so any and all government administrators are held accountable to the needs and interests of its citizenry. Through the process of building an effective Resistance, we will establish a strong, emancipatory, and participatory democracy, one that incorporates the voice of the people in a genuine way.

When we understand the theory and history of nonviolent action, we realize that a victorious people's movement must include a broad range of actions and techniques. Methods of disruption, coercion, and noncompliance are as important as marches, rallies, and contacting elected representatives. What is missing with Indivisible, as with all other Resistance groups currently operating, is a clear understanding of what it truly takes to force a government party and its leader to either radically alter its policies or step down. This book lays out the theory and practical steps required to build a Resistance that has a real chance of meeting its goals.

Outline of the Chapters

Appreciating what inspired today's Resistance, it's important to first look at how Trump and the right-wing extremists are jeopardizing our democracy, the welfare of our people, and the health of our environment so we come to recognize any threats now and in the future. Our immediate concern, then, is in stopping the damage being done by our current administration and preventing such dangerous acts from being repeated by their successors. Chapter One explores the various ways in which Trump and his supporters are threatening the fundamental principles of our democracy and rolling back many of the gains we have made toward equity, diversity, and environmental sustainability.

Nonviolent action has a long and impressive history, dating back to ancient Roman society. Chapter Two discusses how different groups and movements define and practice nonviolent action. While Gandhi and King take an ethical approach to nonviolent action, a foremost authority on nonviolent action and founder of the Albert Einstein Institution, Gene Sharp, takes a practical approach. Each has its strengths and weaknesses and, thus, this book offers a third alternative that builds on the benefits and addresses the drawbacks of both. Regardless of the approach, nonviolent action presupposes a *consent* theory of power. Chapter Three looks at what this is and what the implications are for building a successful people's movement based on this theory.

Chapter Four moves away from the relatively theoretical discussion of nonviolent action into a more practical explanation of its multiple methods and techniques. Here we see what nonviolent action looks like in practice with examples of its use and explanations of what it entails. One of the goals in this chapter is to provide useful information about how people power movements, such as today's Resistance, can put together an effective campaign that tailor specific actions with particular objectives. Following this is an explanation of the different types of changes such movements can lead to, from convincing people they ought to change to creating situations that make it extremely costly for people to not alter their behavior and policies.

Developing a resistance effective enough to shift power relations in society and in governments necessitates a great deal of strategizing and organization. Chapters Five and Six focus primarily on today's Resistance and seek to offer suggestions on how it can grow and strengthen by looking at the theory, methods, and history of nonviolent action discussed in the first chapters of the book. Five discusses the importance of strategic planning as well as the vital necessity of having leaders of the entire movement. The final chapter looks at how the Resistance can shift the balance of power away from Trumpists into the hands of leaders who will better represent the needs of the people. It also explores the idea that the Resistance can lead to more permanent structural changes in our government and society so that demagogues such as Trump and his crony capitalist supporters can never take this country hostage again.

Chapter One
Reasons for Resisting

Protect Our Democracy

If we are to be a government of, by, and for the people, we must have three major things.

1. We need elected officials who will make the people's needs a priority.
2. We also need societal leaders who effectively counter oppressive policies and attitudes.
3. Finally, we need societal structures that enable citizens to voice their needs in ways that cannot be ignored.

When governors are bought and paid for by corporate interests, when they care more about their own power and financial wealth than the people, we don't have a functioning democracy. Instead, we have a system slipping into oligarchy at best and fascism at worst. We have a system where the corrupt and self-serving line their pockets and try selling it to the public as common sense economics, where they strip away rights and protections of minority populations and call it American self-sufficiency, and where they allow the destruction of our environment claiming religious truth over science.

Equality of Opportunity

A democracy requires that all have an equal opportunity to help shape the norms and practices of our society. This cannot occur when the concentration of prosperity is in the hands of a very small minority. 90% of Americans see little increase in wealth while the price of housing, education, childcare, and other living expenses continue to climb. The top 10% of Americans have seen a major increase in their wealth over the last thirty years. This has significantly increased the standard of living and wage gap. While this gap closed a bit during Clinton's and Obama's administrations, it has increased greatly with Trump and threatens to become far wider with the new GOP tax policy. In short, the rich are getting much, much richer, and the middle classes are sinking into poverty.

With Trump's crony capitalism, there are no forces to combat this destructive concentration of wealth, and thus the majority of Americans are struggling to get by.[1] In addition, those at the top of the economic food chain have a prevailing influence on how society is structured, the laws that are passed, and the norms that are established. Unless we require the rich to pay their fair share, we cannot hope for a society that takes seriously the needs and interests of working-class and poor Americans.

Voting

Perhaps more fundamentally, we cannot hope to have a functioning democracy when voting rights are manipulated and suppressed. Republicans continue to pass laws that make it increasingly difficult for people to vote, particularly those who typically vote Democrat: poor, working class, students, and persons of color. From voter fraud suppression, purging voter rolls, and gerrymandering, Republicans have done too much to jeopardize our election process, and we must therefore resist them by insisting that our voting is free and fair.

Voter Fraud Suppression

Republicans have introduced legislation they claim is aimed at reducing voter fraud. The initial problem with this is that there has never been shown to be a problem with voter fraud despite expensive investigations and research meant to reveal it. Therefore, any attempt to suppress voter fraud, such as requiring IDs, should be viewed as suspect. It predominantly impacts the poor, elderly, and physically challenged populations who often don't have and cannot easily acquire one.

Purging Voter Rolls

Purging voter rolls is another attempt to keep the culturally disenfranchised from voting. In a case reported on by journalist Greg Palast in his documentary, "The Best Democracy Money Can Buy," [2] over 7 million people, predominantly people of color from Republican held states, were on a "cross check" list which was a list of people who were suspected of voting multiple times. Palast found that, although over 1 million of these people were removed from their official voter rolls, none were ever prosecuted for their alleged felonies and none matched the criteria that was said to have put them on the list: having the same first, last, and middle names as other voters as well as the same last four digits of their social security numbers.

Gerrymandering

Gerrymandering is another pernicious attempt to unfairly control voting results. The United States is one of the few democracies in the world to employ partisan election managers. Democrats and Republicans in 33 US states have the ability to draw voting district lines to favor their political party. This partisan favoring is so extreme in some cases that their districting has been overturned in court. In

Pennsylvania, for example, according to the *NY Times*,[3] the state Supreme Court ruled that the congressional map constituted a case of unlawful partisan gerrymandering, which greatly favored Republicans.

Not all court cases on this issue are won. In North Carolina, a federal court ruled that the districting map was unfairly drawn to support Republicans. However, the Supreme Court ruled in January 2018 that the federal court's decision was to be overturned. [4] Basically, what gerrymandering does is draw voting district lines to determine which geographical populations will send their winning candidates' votes to be counted with all the other districts' winning votes to be tallied as a total for the state.

If Republicans want to draw the maps in their favor, which they do and have, they would make sure that each district had a Republican majority so that the votes coming from each district were Republican. That any partisan group has the authority to draw these maps seems ridiculous; it invites corruption. The right to vote is a basic tenet of our democracy. It must therefore be protected from any undue partisan political tampering.

Checks and Balances

Our country must also be protected from rulers such as Trump who illustrate time and again an alarming contempt for basic democratic processes, such as the necessity of checks and balances in our government. Congress must be free to operate independently from the President without fear of censure or condemnation. The judicial branch needs to be respected as a nonpartisan upholder of our Constitution without being subjected to constant accusations of pandering to party politics when they act contrary to the President's wishes. White House aides and cabinet members ought to be sufficiently knowledgeable and experienced to carry out their duties responsibly to the benefit of the people rather than the selfish and uniformed demands of an emotionally needy President. And the people have the right and duty to protest whenever their interests are being overrun by private greed and corrupt power seeking.

Congress

When Trump was elected, many thought and hoped that Congress would effectively counter Trump's outrageous and unbalanced behavior. Lifetime Republicans spoke with certainty that Congress would never dare touch Social Security or Medicare for fear of losing the support of seniors, and yet that is precisely what Speaker Ryan is advocating in order to cover the massive increase in the budget deficit caused by the GOP tax bill. While we have seen some definite divisions within the Republican party preventing them from easily passing legislation around such issues as DACA and the Mexican wall, Congress is nevertheless failing to rebuke Trump for his dangerous and unpredictable behavior.

Not only does Congress too often obediently cater to Trump's uninformed demands, they refuse to call him out for violating standard ethical practices and even the law. For example, Congress fails to censure Trump for using his office to promote the Trump brand. They don't hold him to account for holding private meetings with Putin and refusing to impose sanctions against Putin's government. They stood idly by while Trump continuously attempted to defile the reputation of the FBI and other US intelligence agencies. And they did nothing when Trump appeared to have engaged in obstructing justice by firing James Comey and trying to degrade the reputation of Robert Mueller.

Judicial System

In what appears to be a self-deluded belief that he is running an empire, Trump continues to try subverting the independence of the judicial system. He issues Executive Orders, such as his ban on immigrants, that defy the Constitution and then publicly belittles the judges who rule against him. He persists in attacking the reputation of the FBI, firing Director James Comey and questioning the integrity of head of Special Counsel investigation on Russian interference, Robert Mueller. He openly criticized Attorney General Jeff Sessions for being too weak to stop the Russia investigation. And without even consulting DOJ lawyers, he pardoned former Sheriff Arpaio who was convicted of criminal contempt in his dealings with immigrants. Trump's actions reveal his indifference to the rule of law and the importance of checks to a President's power in a constitutional democracy.

Admiration of Dictators

Trump's open admiration for ruthless authoritarians, such as Egypt's Sisi, Philippine's Duterte, North Korea's Kim Jung Un, and Russian's Putin is another reason for concern. As Kenneth Roth, Executive Director of Human Rights Watch, claimed, Trump is a threat to human rights because he is not susceptible to being shamed by moral arguments; rather, he seeks the approval of autocratic rulers.[5] In March 2018, Trump supposedly "joked" at a fundraising event when he said that the US should follow China's model and have a president "for life."[6] More recently, in June 2018, he praised Kim Jung Un for being the "strong head" of his country. Trump was quoted as saying that KJU's "people sit up at attention. I want my people to do the same."[7] He illustrated his desire to be unquestioningly obeyed and admired like these dictators when he made the accusation of treason to all who did not applaud him during his 2018 State of the Union speech. This illustrates not only his complete ignorance of how serious such an accusation is, but it shows his inability to understand how a democracy operates and his unwillingness to support vital democratic rights and freedoms.

Informed Citizenry

Checks and balances to government authority are also required from citizens, who must be free to express opposition to government policies and laws. Our democracy, then, relies on an informed citizenry. Schools need to prepare students to be knowledgeable, skilled, and active participants, and our news media needs to inform us of important local, national, and worldwide events. Unfortunately, just after Trump was elected, a website entitled "Professors Watchlist" was created by a conservative organization intent on naming and shaming professors that the site's organizer, Matt Lamb, claims are promoters of leftist propaganda.[8] Also, with the advent of "alternative facts" and "fake news," it is becoming incredibly difficult for the media to inform the public.

Too many people live in what has been termed an "echo chamber," a place where they only receive information via social media or other biased news sources that tell them what they want to hear. Worse, they receive what appears to be news but what is, instead, misinformation and outright lies meant to appear as legitimate and trustworthy.

Trump has waged a successful war on truth. We see this when Trump labels anything he doesn't want to be true as "fake news" and opposes it with a record-breaking amount of lies.[9] We see it when Press Secretary Sarah Huckabee Sanders backs him up as do other White House aides and right-wing media outlets such as Fox News and Breitbart. We also see it when our elected officials hire people with little to no professional or educational background in top cabinet positions. And we see it when many in Trump's administration ignore the evidence and warnings of scientific, economic and other experts in favor of their own uninformed and non-evidentiary claims.

A democracy cannot thrive when people we entrust to provide us with an accurate picture of current events not only manipulate the truth to serve their own interests but argue that facts are no more important than subjective opinions. A war on truth allows such claims as, "Global warming is not real," "Obama was not born in the United States," and "Supply-side economics helps working class people," to be considered every bit as real, factual, and truthful as their opposing claims. This is absurd. Two opposite statements cannot both be true at the same time. Barring parallel universes, Obama cannot both have been born in the US and not have been born in the US. And only one of those claims is backed up with ample and well-supported evidence.

To believe Obama was not born in the US is to believe a lie, one told and retold by prominent politicians and some celebrities, and to hold that the lie is every bit as acceptable as the truth means we are developing a citizenry who is learning to believe they can pick and choose what to accept and what to reject based solely on who says it or what they want to believe. Evidence, well-supported reasoning, and rational argumentation mean less and less in today's war on truth. Unless we stop this war, we cannot have an informed citizenry, one capable of participating in the democratic process where they make decisions that benefit not only themselves but are mindful and compassionately knowledgeable about the needs of others.

Democracy involves an active and educated populace engaged in the political processes of passing laws and policies, of voicing their needs and being heard, and of effectively resisting governors who seek to limit or take away these democratic rights and freedoms. When the people are active participants in the process of continually formulating and developing the sort of society in which we all want to live, it acts as an important check on the power of the rulers. When our government agencies and their bureaucratic leaders see themselves apart from and above the people, they are susceptible to the greed and corruption that comes with such unchecked power. Their decisions are not sufficiently shaped by, and thus do not adequately reflect, the needs of the people. The democratic process involves communities of inquiry engaged in problem solving that takes into account the experiences and interests of all

11

groups. No one group can decide for others what is best for them. Rather, decisions that affect our daily lives must be made via this democratic process. Currently, too many of our lawmakers are ignoring their constituents' needs and wants in favor of their own private interests. We see this when laws to protect Dreamers and reasonable gun safety laws fail to pass even though an overwhelming majority of the American people supports such legislation.

On a global scale, our democracy is threatened when our government adopts authoritarian and oppressive international policies where women and people of color don't receive the beneficial protections that white men do and where policies unfairly favor the wealthy over the poor and middle classes. No nation lives in isolation; our country's actions on the world stage affect our own cultural practices and attitudes.

The US is not alone in its move toward more authoritarian rulers. Trump's empowerment of such political views, of hateful and oppressive attitudes and actions, of demonizing the free press, and of enriching the top 1% at the crippling cost to working peoples is spreading. This Trumpism is also seen in the cavalier and ignorant view of the health of our world. We cannot have a democracy when the planet on which we depend for our lives is not protected. Bottom line, democracy fails when Trumpism reigns supreme and our governors refuse to represent the people for whom they were elected to work.

**Safeguard Human Rights
(and 14th Amendment Protections)**

When a government either engages in acts that jeopardize the basic human rights of its people or refuses to take reasonable steps to protect them, the people need to demand change. Racism, sexism, transphobia, homophobia, and religious and ethnic intolerance are not new in the United States. They are as old as the country itself. While we continue to make strides forward, sometimes our progress is unacceptably slow, sometimes it seems not to be moving at all, and in some cases, it moves backwards. Today, too many in our government are allowing us to lose the progress we have fought so hard to gain, and some are outright pushing us backwards. What we see today is a combination of rhetoric and actions that are re-defining the US as a white supremacist nation determined to keep people of color oppressed by the white power holders, women under control by the patriarchy, and Christianity as the dominant religion.

<u>Immigrants and Religious Minorities</u>
The laws that the government has passed and is trying to pass are jeopardizing the human rights of oppressed minorities. On January 27, only one week after he took office, Trump signed an executive order preventing any person from entering the US from seven Muslim-majority

nations for 90 days and any refugee from all countries for 120 days. Although Trump tried justifying his ban, stating that the seven countries (Iran, Iraq, Libya, Somalia, Sudan, Syria, and Yemen) were home to the most extreme Islamic terrorists, he failed to explain why this list did not include Egypt, Lebanon, Saudi Arabia, and the United Arab Emirates where the 9/11 terrorist were from. Trump and his Chief of Staff Reince Priebus justified their list by claiming that Obama identified these seven nations.

While it is true that Obama identified these nations, Obama did not issue a total ban; instead, according to PolitiFact,[10] he required people visiting from these countries to have a visa. It takes more than supposition that anyone entering the US from a given country is a security risk to issue a total ban, which is why the courts ruled Trump's ban illegal. Furthermore, the ban prevented entry of refugees even though there is no evidence that they are a danger to US security. In fact, Trump put pressure on his administration to reject the findings of a study by the Department of Homeland Security that refugees in the US over the past ten years brought in $63 billion more than they cost.[11]

Trump's willingness to sacrifice the wellbeing of vulnerable groups is shared by many in the GOP who put the future of millions in jeopardy by using funding for CHIP and protections for Dreamers as political leverage rather than passing favorable legislation for these programs they overwhelmingly said they support. Trump and his Congress spread false narratives about immigrants stealing jobs from Americans, taking advantage of America's welfare system, not paying taxes, and causing most of the terrorist crimes. These lies feed into the fears of those looking for scapegoats for their economic and personal despair. Trump supporters ignore facts; they ignore that immigrants bring in millions of dollars more than they cost, that their crime rates are far lower than those who have lived here for generations, and that they fulfill social and economic roles deeply needed in our country.

LGBTQ Community

Immigrants are not the only group at risk under the Trump administration. Trump has made it far easier for health care providers to discriminate against members of the LGBTQ community. For example, in January 2018, Trump created a division within the Health and Human Services (HHS) department that oversees medical professionals' right to refuse treatment for religious reasons. This directive follows others aimed at trans people, such as the so-called "bathroom bill" that revoked protections for trans students using the bathroom corresponding to their gender identity. Additionally, Trump proposed a ban on transgendered folks from serving in the military. Trump's vice-president is also a threat to LGBTQ people by citing God in his crusade to

15

oppose gay marriage and legalize conversion therapy. Right-wing advocates have jumped on this new political justification for discrimination and have targeted members of the LGBTQ community by refusing gay couples services such as those by photographers, hair salons, reception halls, and bakers. It has gotten so bad that even some students of social work are expressing a wish to deny service to gay people.[12]

People of Color

In addition to immigrants and members of the LGBTQ community, the Trump administration is hostile to people of color. A few examples will help illustrate the blatant racism coming out of the Trump administration. Trump and Melania championed the false narrative that Obama was not born in the US. Trump and his supporters justify the existence of Confederate monuments. Trump himself called Mexicans rapists and thieves and insists on building a massively expensive wall on the Mexican border. He referred to Senator Elizabeth Warren as Pocahontas when speaking to a group of Navajo Code Talkers. In one of his too many ignorant posts on Twitter, Trump re-tweeted an anti-Muslim meme from a right-wing extremist hate group in Britain. He continues to show a lack of concern over Puerto Ricans' suffering from the hurricane disaster. He berates Colin Kaepernick and others for their take-a-knee movement to call for safe and equal treatment of blacks by law enforcement. And he referred to El Salvador, Haiti, and African countries as "shitholes." These are just some of the ways in which Trump has shown that he cares very little about protecting the rights and freedoms of black and brown people.

In December 2015, he unabashedly raised anti-Semitic stereotypes when he likened himself to Jews by claiming he too had masterful financial negotiation skills. Then in 2017, during a rally in Charlottesville, VA, where one of the lead speakers, Robert "Azzmador" Ray, declared "Death to the enemies of the white race!", Trump said that there were some "very fine people." These "very fine people" were at a rally organized for months as a militaristic event with the aim of declaring war on any who oppose white supremacy. And one of these very fine individuals purposely drove his car into Heather Heyer, a peaceful protestor who subsequently died as a result.

Women

Finally, Trump and his supporters show that they have little regard for the respectful treatment of women. Although many called Trump out for bragging about getting away with sexually assaulting women, which was caught on video, he was still voted in and supported by the majority in the GOP. Putting aside all the degrading remarks and actions he's made and reported to have committed against women before taking office, such as publicly claiming that he'd date Ivanka if she wasn't his daughter and stating in an interview with *New York Magazine* that men have to treat women like "shit",[13] there is plenty to concern ourselves with during his time as a presidential candidate and as POTUS.

His treatment of Hillary Clinton alone tells us all we need to know about his abusive, bullying, and degrading demeanor toward women, especially those who dare stand up to him. His comment to journalist Megyn Kelly is further proof of his hatred of strong women when he said she must be having her period when she questioned him on his misogynistic comments. Against women who accused him of sexual misconduct, he tried defending himself on one occasion by claiming the woman was too ugly for him to have sexually harassed her. On Twitter, he again tried shaming a woman for her looks when he wrote that he refused to meet with *Morning Joe*'s Mika Brzezinski because "She was bleeding badly from a face-lift."[14] And again on Twitter, in an obvious attempt at sexual shaming, he wrote that Senator Kristen Gillibrand "would do anything" for a campaign contribution from Trump.[15]

Although words from the President of the US matter in that they set the tone for how many feel they can behave, we should also look at Trump's actions against women. In his first week as POTUS, Trump repealed by executive order Obama's reversal of the Global Gag Rule, a policy that doesn't allow the US to fund any international organization that provides abortions, even though they do provide essential health care to millions of women worldwide. The Trump administration also attacked women's reproductive rights by trying to defund Planned Parenthood and other American family planning organizations that provide critical health care needs for women.

In January 2018, Trump made it easier for doctors to refuse to perform abortions under the special department he set up in the department of Health and Human Services. Trump appointed Charmaine Yoest to lead this department as assistant secretary of public affairs. Prior to this post, she was head of the prominent anti-abortion group, Americans United for Life.[16] Trump's Vice President Pence tried taking away maternity care from insurance policies as a trade-off for taking the ACA repeal bill from the White House to Congress.

The combination of Trump's degrading and abusive comments to and about women with his and his administration's attack on women's reproductive rights and health care, show that he is a threat to women's equality and general wellbeing. In addition, his administration jeopardizes the welfare of people from other oppressed groups: immigrants, members of the LGBTQ community, people of color, and non-Christian minorities. When a democratic government fails to protect the life, liberty, and happiness of their people, particularly those who are most vulnerable, the people have a duty to fight for their democratic and human rights.

Ensure an Environmentally Sustainable Future

Trump and his right-wing supporters have shown little regard for the environment. From their direct attacks on the EPA, their refusal to listen to the scientific community, and their repeal of vital protections, they have illustrated that corporate interests prevail over any consideration of the welfare of our planet. Putting the oil industry and other beneficiaries of crony capitalism above the wellbeing of the environment spells disaster for the improving and even maintaining of our drinking water, air quality, biodiversity, and sustainable land use.

<u>Climate Change</u>
The first act that spelled doom for environmentalists and all who recognize the need to institute reasonable laws that protect our natural world was Trump's appointment of Scott Pruitt as head of the EPA. Pruitt was Attorney General of Oklahoma and repeatedly fought against the EPA. According to a *Washington Post* article, Pruitt has spent much of his career trying to overturn EPA regulations that would limit the expulsion of greenhouse gases and has

claimed that global warming is still a debate among scientists that is "far from settled."[17] As a climate change denier and advocate of big business over environmental interests, Pruitt was a warning sign that the Trump administration would try to end the Obama era environmental protections and regulations.

Since then, the Trump administration has done a great deal to show they intend to overturn many of our existing environmental protection policies. In June 2017, for example, Trump decided to pull out of the Paris Climate agreement, breaking away from 194 other countries that agreed to do what they could to reduce their countries' greenhouse gas emissions. In October 2017, the Trump administration deleted several links from the EPA website that provided officials with information on how to deal with global warming; pages were deleted that discussed how states could address climate change. Only two months later, the Trump administration told the Center for Disease Control that they could not use certain words in official documents, *science-based* and *evidence-based* being two of the seven words prohibited. Far easier to deny climate change if science and factual evidence have no more weight than biased belief and political expediency. In fact, Trump took climate change off the list of national security risks.

Protection of Animals

The welfare of animals is also not a priority for Trump and the GOP. In December 2017, Trump's Interior Department announced that companies would no longer be held legally accountable for indirectly causing the death of birds. Thus, corporate America no longer has to concern itself with their oil spills or power lines spaced too close together.[18] Causing even further outrage from environmentalists, animal rights activists, and many public citizens, Trump and Congress voted to lift the ban on hunting and killing wolves in their dens and hibernating bears. Such acts seem unnecessarily cruel as does releasing the ban against trophy hunting of elephants and lions, species that may go extinct if their pointless slaughter is not prevented. Trump is more interested in pleasing hunters than saving our wildlife.

Protection of Land

In addition to animals, Trump has shown little regard for the protection and welfare of our land, on and offshore. In August 2017, Trump signed an executive order overturning Obama's policy that required federally funded projects to adhere to certain flood risk standards. To add insult to injury, Trump's policies that threaten the environment indicate that he shows unfair favoritism when he, himself, may be harmed. In his proposed plan announced in January 2018 that will allow for far more US coastline oil drilling, he exempted Florida where his "second White House" Mar-a-

Lago is located. Although the majority of governors of coastal states object to offshore oil drilling (with the exception of Maine, Alabama, Alaska, and Mississippi), according to a CNN online article, Trump only gave a waiver to Florida.[19] In protest against the coastal drillings, the majority of the National Parks System Advisory Board resigned as a group in January 2018, citing Trump's continual disregard for science, climate change, and environmental health. The Board members were also appalled by the Trump administration's historic move to reduce the largest amount of land, approximately two million acres, from federal protection.

In addition to national Parks members, Trump alarmed the solar industry when he approved policies that would tax foreign made solar equipment by as much as 30 percent.[20] The solar companies depend on overseas manufacturers for the majority of their equipment. Given the higher prices for parts and supplies, solar companies fear they won't be able to meet their projected production needs. Thus, layoffs will likely occur by as many as 23,000 jobs. These taxes and layoffs mean higher prices for solar power, which means fewer people opting for solar. To protect our environment, our country needs to continue to advance in green energy technology and make it more available to people. Reducing the likelihood that Americans will convert to solar energy means more dependence on big oil and less on alternative, green sources of power.

Trump and right-wing extremists have provided a long list of reasons to resist. From safeguarding the dignity, equality, and liberty of all Americans, to protecting our environment, and fortifying our democratic rights and freedoms, the Resistance continues to fight against a government that shows a dangerously increasing tendency to choose Party affiliation over fundamental democratic principles and basic human decency. When a majority of our governors turn their backs on the people they were elected to represent and jeopardize the wellbeing of the people, the environment, and the proper functioning of our democracy, and when such governors spread the harmful impacts of Trumpism, it is time for the people to resist.

We have a window of opportunity now to act. The Resistance is strong and highly motivated; we cannot afford to lose that momentum by delaying. We also cannot afford to wait to protect our environment. According to scientists, we are currently experiencing mass extinctions, and we have only a limited time to take corrective action before the very survival of the human species is put in jeopardy.[21] Supporting today's Resistance and building a people's movement to build structures that hold future leaders accountable is vital to maintaining our democracy and safeguarding our planet.

What Kind of Democracy are We Fighting For?

When in the Course of human events it becomes necessary for one people to dissolve the political bands which have connected them with another ... they should declare the causes which impel them to the separation ... Governments are instituted among [people], deriving their just powers from the consent of the governed, — That whenever any Form of Government becomes destructive of these ends, it is the Right of the People to alter or to abolish it, and to institute new Government, laying its foundation on such principles and organizing its powers in such form, as to them shall seem most likely to affect their Safety and Happiness."[22]

When a government, any government, substitutes their own private interests for the will of the people, we as democratic citizens have the right to take away their power and replace it with people, policies, laws, and decision-making structures that better address the needs of the people. On Trump's one-year anniversary, for the first time in US history, the government shut down when it was controlled in the House, Senate, and White House by one political party. This, along with the legislation being introduced and passed that threatens our democracy, threatens the health of our planet, and brings the nation dangerously backwards in terms of promoting human rights are all very strong reasons to demand better of our government.

The Resistance is not simply working to replace Republicans with Democrats. Rather, they seek to put into office people who will sustain our democratic principles, safeguard our human rights, and help ensure future generations can enjoy life on a sustainable planet. The Resistance needs to fight for a government that truly represents us, in actions not just in lip-service. Building a people's movement that effectively challenges the power of our government takes a great deal of work, training, and organization; yet, it is our right and arguably our duty as democratic citizens to resist government leaders who are a direct threat to the very foundations of our democracy.

Nonviolent resistance campaigns require active participation by a massive number of people from a broad range of cultural, social, and political groups. The structures they set up, therefore, tend to be representative of a broad range of interest groups. They also tend to be participatory, primarily because it's the best way to get things done. For a group to continue to motivate its members, those members must be given a say in how the group operates and the goals they are working toward. As Dewey argued, a democracy is

> more than a form of government; it is primarily a mode of associated living, of conjoint communicated experience. The extension in space of the number of individuals who

participate in an interest so that each has to refer his own action to that of others, and to consider the action of others to give point and direction to his own, is equivalent to the breaking down of those barriers of class, race, and national territory which kept men from perceiving the full import of their activity.[23]

This is what a resistance campaign helps create, a collection of diverse groups working together on common causes with shared goals. It, therefore, supports a democracy in two very important ways. It develops organizations necessary for running and sustaining a democratic society, and it provides an effective means for empowering the people so their demands are heard and acted upon.

If we understand democracy to mean a government by, for, and of the people, then we mean a participatory and emancipatory rather than a merely representative government. The framers of our US Constitution considered it a fair and just move to replace autocracy, where a small group of people have virtually unlimited power and rarely if ever have to consult the will of the people, with a form of governance that involved the consent of the people. It is this *consent* that is fundamental to our freedom. Without it, we do not have a government accountable to the welfare of its people.

Although our forbearers were influenced by political philosopher John Locke's contractual notion of governance, they promoted a more representational form of democracy. Yet, there were those who envisioned a more participatory democracy, one that meets better with the spirit of Locke's views centered around the idea of consent. Put simply, Locke argued that a government is essentially a group of people who pass laws that, in effect, restrict a people's freedom to do whatever they want. It imposes an order that converts our lives from those of wild savages, continually fighting each other for survival, to a society with rules that protect our overall lives, happiness, and freedom to pursue the goals we choose. To ensure that a government does not pass laws that jeopardize our life, liberty, and pursuit of happiness, Locke purposed that there be a contract between the people and government. This contract outlines the powers of the government. [24]

In the US, that contract is the Constitution. As with any contract, all interested parties have the right to ensure that it is followed. One popular view of our democracy is that the people elect politicians whose job it is to honor the terms of the contract. Another popular view, one advocated in this book, is that the entire purpose of the contract is to ensure that the needs of the people are met by those they elect into government. If they are not, the people have a right to either insist the elected officials follow the contract or amend it to better serve the interests of the people. Such a view precludes the notion of a democracy as a process whereby citizens' primary role is not to engage in decision-making but to merely elect others who will. It is further stipulated in this conception of democracy that all adult citizens have an *equal* opportunity to participate in the decision-making processes. Without it, our government can hardly be said to represent the needs of its entire people or to have their consent in taking the actions they do.

Consent is something that must be given. It cannot be assumed that a people will agree to the rules and policies others impose on them. Just as women's experiences reveal that men do not fully understand them and thus don't always act in their interests, the same goes for men not being fully understood by women. Additionally, black and brown people have similar experiences in regards to white people, Jews and Muslims to Christians, and so on. Unlike political philosopher John Rawls's veil of ignorance[25] where anyone can address the needs of anyone else in society by simply imagining oneself in the other's place, we know from our own experiences that no one can speak for us better than we can. Thus, a participatory and emancipatory democracy entails not only that all people have the opportunity to participate in meaningful decisions but also that they have an *equal* opportunity to do so.

Equality of opportunity is far from a simple goal. Rather, it requires a long and dedicated commitment to empowering oppressed groups. Strategic nonviolent action is designed to do this because it restructures power relations. In any successful nonviolent campaign for justice, the organization and leadership of the movement must derive from the people themselves. Prominent writer on the theory and methods of strategic nonviolent action, Gene Sharp, is very careful to point out that neither he nor anyone else can decide for a people how to develop or run their campaign. To do so would be to replace one set of rulers with another.

Often times, a major source of problems with corrupt rulers is that the decision-making structure is itself faulty, and this would not be altered if one group of leaders were merely replaced by another. Trumpism, in other words, will not disappear with the election of more enlightened leaders. While better leaders will certainly help tremendously, Trump and the right-wing has initiated and formed corrupt structures that allow selfish and sometimes even cruel policies and actions to continue even after he is gone. What we need for a true participatory and emancipatory democracy to flourish is to create organizational systems wherein the people play a significantly meaningful role in making decisions about the sort of society in which we all choose to live. Strategic nonviolent action is a proven way to both oppose autocratic authority and build societal structures that promote economic and socio-political equity.

To better understand how strategic nonviolent action

works and how today's Resistance can utilize its techniques, we need to learn what nonviolent action is. What follows, then, is a discussion of the theory of its effectiveness, its various methods, how it has been used in multiple historical examples, and how today's Resistance can employ it. Learning about nonviolent action will help us build a Resistance campaign that can shut down the Trump administration and replace it with a governing system that truly represents the needs and the will of the people.

Chapter Two
Understanding Nonviolent Action

Outside academic circles, *nonviolent action* is not a term familiar to many in the United States. Although most people have a general understanding that it involves a nonviolent approach to resolving conflict, many are not aware that when it is used to take on an entire government or the foundational structures of a society, it involves as much organization and strategic planning as a violent war. Like war, it involves trained and knowledgeable leaders, willing and courageous foot soldiers, and a wide range of weapons designed to serve many different purposes.

By understanding the theory of nonviolent action, Resisters can learn how to alter the balance of power between government leaders and the people. Learning about the hundreds of different techniques and their purposes will help Resisters select the best techniques to meet their objectives. And reading about various resistance movements throughout history will teach Resisters about the organization required to be successful. Gaining a more thorough knowledge of what nonviolent action is and how it's been used in history, the Resistance can build on current successes and create a more powerful movement that can effectively take down Trump and counter the future impact he has. Additionally, it can build diverse societal structures that empower all people to participate in decisions that affect their daily lives.

I use the term *nonviolent action* (NVA) instead of *nonviolence* because the latter is too often taken to mean the mere absence of violence. Nonviolent action is, first and foremost, *action*. It is organized and strategic action that does not employ violence toward others and is used for the purpose of opposing injustice. For a clearer understanding, it is helpful to distinguish it from similar concepts that often get conflated and confused with NVA, such as pacifism, civil resistance, and civil disobedience. These are distinct yet related to NVA as are the actions of negotiation, diplomacy, and conflict resolution. I examine each of these to not only help clarify what nonviolent action is, but also to emphasize the importance of strategy, leadership, structure, and training. While most resistance movements develop from small, community grass-roots groups protesting certain rules and advocating for particular changes, those that are successful involve nearly as much planning, courage, and organization as violent war.

What Nonviolent Action is Not

<u>Negotiation, Diplomacy, Conflict Resolution</u>
To start with the most straightforward distinctions, NVA does not involve negotiations, diplomacy, or conflict resolution; rather, these processes are tried *before* NVA is employed. Negotiation is the art of two opposing parties engaging in dialogue to reach a compromise for the purpose of ending an existing or threatened conflict. Diplomacy involves working with foreign leaders and representatives to arrive at agreements that prevent violent engagements. Finally, conflict resolution is an umbrella term that includes methods of negotiation, diplomacy, anger management, forgiveness training, and many others aimed at reaching an agreement that avoids violent conflict. Because NVA is an active form of struggle between opposing groups, it is only initiated once all efforts at resolving the conflict have been tried and failed.

As with violent war, NVA is a set of methods that involve organization, training, strategizing, commitment, and discipline, and it is ideally used only after negotiations, diplomacy, and other forms of conflict resolution have proven ineffective. Although it is ideal if resolutions can be achieved through peaceful forms of discussion, where opposing parties come to an agreement on mutually beneficial compromises, that doesn't always happen. When it does not occur, there needs to be an alternative.

Violence is one common alternative. We see it on school playgrounds, between rival street gangs, and in civil and international wars. Nonviolent action is another common alternative. We see it with continual whining and nagging, shunning, dogging people, labor strikes, massive peaceful protest marches, organized boycotts, work-to-rule actions, student walkouts, foot dragging, and so on. Because both violent and nonviolent actions are costly to both participants and opponents, they should try to be avoided through methods of peaceful conflict resolution. When such methods fail, however, nonviolent action proves to be less costly and more effective than violence.

Civil Disobedience

Civil disobedience involves participants disobeying rules for the purposes of both exposing an injustice and putting pressure on the opposition to change the rules. When done effectively, it is strategically planned action in which participants anticipate backlash and reprisals, carry out responsive actions to those reprisals, and prepare support for participants who may suffer losses as a result of their actions. For example, Gandhi always appointed people to take over should he be arrested and sent to jail, which he often was. Although much more will be said about this category of methods, it is important here to note that civil disobedience is distinct from NVA in that the latter is the name for the entire range of methods used in a peaceful movement, whereas the former names only those methods that involve strategic disobedience or noncooperation.

Pacifism

Pacifism is a moral or philosophical outlook, sometimes but not always adopted by those who practice and advocate for NVA. Often times NVA is mistaken for pacifism. When I tell people that I don't support violent war, they assume I'm a pacifist. They assume, in other words, that I have a moral objection to violent wars. The truth is that I do and don't. I do because I believe there is a viable alternative. However, I wouldn't have a moral objection if I thought wars were, at least in some cases, the only way to stop a terrible injustice. Pacifists, unlike myself, are not concerned with the expediency of war; they are focused only on its ethical considerations.

Philosopher Douglas Lackey[1] points out that not all pacifists hold the same views about violence. While some believe that all violence is wrong, others only admonish the intentional taking of another's life. Still others believe that violence only in the personal sphere is wrong but is sometimes justified in war. Conversely, some believe that war is morally indefensible but there are occasions when violence in one's personal life is justified. This latter form of pacifism is what most people think of when someone claims to be against war. Yet, even this form of pacifism is distinct from those who support NVA.

If we look at war from an ethical standpoint, some pacifists may support it and others wouldn't, depending on what view of pacifism they hold. Regardless, their views would be based exclusively on their moral stance of violence in war. NVA advocates may also oppose war on ethical grounds. However, they don't oppose it because the violence in war is wrong in and of itself. Rather, it is wrong because it can realistically be avoided with a credible substitute. Other supporters of NVA oppose war for reasons of expediency. They disregard moral arguments about war and focus instead on the practical success of NVA. For them, violent war is far less likely to end in victory and its costs are immensely high, making NVA a far better option.

Civil Resistance

The term *civil resistance* is very closely related to the term *nonviolent action*. In fact, they are often used synonymously. Kurt Schock's book *Civil Resistance Today*,[2] for example, discusses the same or very similar theoretical and practical underpinnings covered in books on nonviolent action. And Stellan Vinthagen's *A Theory of Nonviolent Action: How Civil Resistance Works*[3] equates the two terms. Yet, I think there is a subtle but very important distinction, one found more in practice than in theoretical discussions. The distinction centers on the terms *resistance* versus *action*. The term *resistance* places emphasis on the act of resisting and does not necessarily place an equal focus on

37

building and restructuring. The notion of NVA, on the other hand, does exactly that.

While resistance is a form of action, it implies a negating or opposing of certain policies, structures, and practices. It does not necessarily imply a creating of alternative structures and relations. Today's Resistance, for example, started out and is still primarily focused on opposing the Trump agenda. Many of today's groups are ad hoc; they are meant to address the immediate concern of Trump and right-wing extremism rather than form a lasting people power system that acts as an effective check on the power of all government officials. What the Resistance lacks is a strategy to build power relations where people have a stronger voice in the decisional processes and where elected officials are held more accountable to the people.

Understanding the Notion of Violence

The term *nonviolent* isn't ideal because it's a negative term. It mandates what to avoid but does not mandate what to do. This is why it may be preferable to use the words *civil* action or *peaceful* action. I use nonviolent because civil action most often indicates an official complaint made against another in a court of law. The term peaceful action is good because it promotes something positive: peace. The problem with this, though, is that *peace* connotes a sense of serenity and inner calm that does not coincide with the more war-like strategic planning and operations of NVA. Additionally, the term nonviolent action has historical precedence with its use by Gene Sharp and Martin Luther King, Jr. However, to understand what nonviolent truly means, we need to gain clarity on what violence is.

<u>Structural Violence</u>
Hitting, shooting, and stabbing - these are what one typically thinks of as violence. Yet, there are other, less visible but just as powerful forms of violence. Structural violence, simply put, is the harm enacted through societal structures. For example, societies are made up of (or structured by) institutions, power hierarchies, policies and laws, norms, traditions, and narratives. These are what keep our society from being a free-for-all where people do whatever they wish. Structures in society help organize it so it operates in a relatively predictable and safe way. We generally know what to expect in our lives from one day to the next. If we quit going to work, we know we'll be fired. If we break the law, we will pay a penalty. If we continually violate what's considered normal social behavior in public, we will likely suffer being ridiculed and ostracized.

We count on structures to make our daily lives comfortable. Yet, when these structures harm people by unjustly privileging some groups over others, such harm is a form of violence. For example, when law enforcement unfairly targets and attacks black men, that is structural violence. There are different forms of structural violence, such as endemic poverty, repeated mass killing, and oppression. I look at each of these three to give a better idea of what structural violence is and to show how pernicious its harms are.

Understanding this form of violence is important for a couple reasons. First, we will see how nonviolent action helps to decrease it. Second, we better appreciate the dangers of Trump and the Trump-effect; we see it as a form of violence that is working its way into the structures of our society. Learning more about structural violence teaches us that we must not only oppose Trump; we must also seek to root out and defeat the lasting impact he will have on our future. Avoiding this sort of violence requires that NVA participants become aware of what structural violence is, learn to recognize it when it occurs, and help form bonds, interconnections, and power relations in society that aid in breaking it down and replacing it with more equitable systems and relationships.

Endemic Poverty

Persistent extreme poverty is one example of structural violence. It occurs when relations of power and the distribution of goods continually recreate patterns of privilege and subjugation. The wealthy institute and enact policies that maintain their position of financial dominance.

Even when marginalized groups break out and establish their own enterprise, expressing views that question and oppose mainstream norms, when they become successful, they are often bought and commodified by the ruling elite. This occurred with the rap music industry. Although it began as a voice of poor, inner city young people of color, predominantly white corporate owned groups took over and became its main beneficiaries.

Repeated Mass Killings

Repeated acts of mass killing are other examples of structural violence. A complex network of intersecting forces helps create societal conditions where individuals feel the best way to be heard is through extreme and hostile action. Lynching in the South is an example of this where too many white people felt threatened by even the smallest amount of freedoms given to black people. Recently, mass shootings in public spaces, schools, and businesses are occurring at disturbingly increasing rates. Granted only a small minority of individuals choose to express their rage and hopelessness by committing such atrocities. Yet, the frequency of these incidents indicates a problem larger than individual instances of psychological maladjustment. Gang fights, violent protests, and mass killings occur with alarming frequency in this country, and we must therefore consider societal factors that may be contributing to such violence.

41

Oppression

Another type of structural violence is oppression in all its forms. It is both omnipresent and often invisible because it is so intricately woven into the very fabric of our society. As such, it is part of our lives from the moment we are born until we pass on into death. What has been present since birth is often seen as normal and even inevitable; it doesn't occur to us to question it. Patriarchy, for example, is a socio-political and economic system where males assume authority over females and persistently benefit at the cost of women's interests in all spheres of life. For too long, it has been viewed as an appropriate and even natural state of relations in society. Yet, a basic contention of feminists is that patriarchy is neither natural nor appropriate.

Feminist peace education scholar, Birgit Brock-Utne claims that the "state of patriarchy is the state of war."[4] She argues that patriarchal societies, where male values are given priority over female values, contribute to a war mentality. This is due to the values themselves (e.g., competition versus cooperation, dominance versus interdependence, and violence versus caring), but it is also due to the power structure. When a society is arranged such that one group is continually privileged at the expense of another, we have a society idealistically and psychologically prepared for subjugation and violent domination.

Oppression occurs against groups in society, and it operates differently for different groups. Formulating a unified and clear conception of oppression, therefore, is quite difficult because it takes on a variety of forms depending upon which group is being affected. Feminist philosopher Iris M. Young addresses this difficulty in her work, giving oppression five "faces:" [5] exploitation, cultural imperialism, marginalization, powerlessness, and violence. Briefly, exploitation occurs when people are not compensated at a fair rate because of the cultural group to which they belong. Paying women less than men for the same job with the same professional experience is an example of exploitation.

Cultural imperialism and marginalization are two sides of the same coin. The former privileges one cultural group's attitudes, values, practices, norms, styles, religion, food, knowledge, experiences, and goals over all others making that one group's culture the norm and the standard by which all other cultures are found wanting. Marginalization occurs when people's habits, life styles, and identities are only allowed to exist in the margins of society because they do not meet the standards of the dominant culture. Requiring that members of the LGBTQ exhibit in public behavior akin to those of cisgendered heterosexuals is an example where one culture has an imperial dominance over others who are, thus, forced to display their cultural norms and narratives in private.

Powerlessness oppression is when people from marginalized cultures have a more difficult time acquiring and maintaining positions of power in society because of the cultural group to which they belong. When women and people of color have to overcome far more obstacles to attain college acceptances, jobs, promotions, and political positions because they are seen as less able than white men, this is an example of powerlessness oppression.

Finally, violence oppression describes the sort of direct and physical violence against people because of the cultural group to which they belong. Attacking Jews or Blacks or Muslims *because* they are Jewish or black or Muslim is violence oppression. All forms of oppression operate against individuals from marginalized cultural groups *because of the group to which they belong*. Thus, if Jennie punches Ben because Ben said hateful things to her, Jennie is violent but not oppressive. If Jennie punches Ben because he is Jewish, she is being violently oppressive. Her violence is not only an attack against Ben as an individual; it is an attack on Jews because, as a Jew, Ben and others are at risk of being victims for no other reason than them being Jewish.

Acts of oppression may look the same as those that are otherwise unfair, unjust, cruel, and hateful, but they only qualify as oppression when a person or persons are behaving toward others who are from marginalized cultural groups because of the group to which they belong. The difference can be seen in more than just the intention of the perpetrator. As a Jew, Ben lives every day with the knowledge that he is a target of hate, mistrust, and violence from many in society.

Structural violence is a continuous state of affairs that can be seen and felt in countless subtle and obvious ways such as casual racist comments by co-workers, stereotyped images in the media, re-interpreting one's motives to fit dominant narratives, discriminatory practices in professional and educational spheres, unfairly harsh treatment by law enforcement, and so on. In the above example of oppression, then, Ben is not just an unfortunate victim of a one-time occurrence of violence (or even multiple occurrences); rather, he is more vulnerable than others to unfair and unjust treatment or the fear of such treatment every day.

Structural violence often works invisibly to unfairly privilege some cultural groups over others, to reduce the agency of entire populations, to have an elite group determine what counts as knowledge for everyone and what meanings and intentions are implied by others' actions and words. It acts to subordinate one's identity for the truncated stereotyped identity assigned by the dominant group. Finally, it is to believe the interests that benefit the powerful benefit all. This highlights the remarkable MeToo movement – grass roots outrage at the longstanding oppression of women. It has made visible what remained invisible and accepted for so long, and as a result, it has taken down powerful men from both political parties and corporate America.

To combat structural violence, resistance groups must first recognize what it is and how it operates. It must then combat it by taking care to have culturally diverse leadership, and to create cooperative relations between different groups in society. Whites and others from positions of power in society need to be mindful to not privilege their perspectives and voices over others when establishing goals for the resistance. If diversity and equal opportunity for participation is built into resistance organizations, new societal structures will be formed that break down unjust barriers of oppression. Put simply, NVA helps people show solidarity and give voice to individuals from a broad spectrum of ideologies and life experiences.

Direct Violence

Aside from physical attacks, direct violence includes verbal threats and the use of obscenities against one's opposition. It's worth noting, however, that activists differ about what constitutes verbal threats and obscenities. In a nonviolent vigil in Manchester, NH where myself and other protestors held signs outside a venue hosting Steven Bannon who was raising funds to support local right-wing and free-state candidates, nonviolence precluded us from physically attacking attendees. However, it was not clear whether it precluded us from yelling things like "shame" or "booo." Organizers of the event did not want us yelling any such negative words and, although we all complied, feeling we owed the organizers our respect by following their guidelines, not all agreed that such utterances constituted violence and, therefore, should not be used. The line between violent and nonviolent verbal behavior then, is not always clear or agreed upon.

Direct Violence as a Result of Structural Violence
Direct violence is much easier to identify than structural violence. However, as we see from the discussion above, it is often the result of structural inequities and injustices in society. Thus, when avoiding direct violence, NVA activists must make sure they do not support structurally violent systems in their efforts to promote justice. For example, people from all genders must be included in promoting gender equity; all racial groups must have an equal say in race relations; and individuals from different faith communities need to be involved in building spiritual support for people in crisis. It is not enough, therefore, for NVA participants to refrain from physical forms of violence against their opposition. They must also be mindful of working to interrupt oppressive and other structurally violent habits and attitudes.

Violence Against One's Self versus Violence Against Others
Participating in NVA means rejecting violent forms of

resistance when directed at one's opponents. However, it does not necessarily require that activists refrain from using or inciting violence against themselves. For example, Vietnamese Buddhist monks' self-immolation[6] to protest the Vietnam War was certainly violent. Similarly, Gandhi's hunger strikes[7] were a violent way to protest against his followers engaging in violence. Alice Paul was also violent when she went on a hunger strike to oppose her unjust imprisonment for protesting women's suffrage.[8] Yet, NVA supports these actions as well as those that put oneself willingly and purposively in harm's way, such as African-American civil rights protestors who willingly subjected themselves to physical harm when they refused to leave the lunch counters designated for Whites only.[9]

In working for positive socio-political change, NVA activists allow direct violence to one's own self when done in the altruistic pursuit of peace and justice, but they do not allow activists to use violence against the opposition. As Gandhi[10] warned his followers when combating the British, his followers may be jailed, tortured, or even killed, but they may not return violence with violence. In other words, in using nonviolent action, one may be the *recipient* of violence, but one must never inflict it on others.

To avoid violence means refraining from the use of physical and verbal harm against one's opponents. It also means being mindful of structural injustice so activists can help subvert systemic and institutional violence. NVA goes beyond merely resisting dangerous policies and practices. It involves replacing current societal power relations with more equitable ones that enable the people to have a much greater say in how society is run, what it values, and how it progresses. Also, because activists sometimes risk their jobs and even their personal safety when taking action against powerful rulers, their work does not fit the serene image of a peaceful endeavor. The term nonviolent action, then, entails methods that are not violent to actively oppose a perceived injustice. Additionally, as defined and practiced by such activists as Gandhi, King, and Sharp, it seeks to obstruct structural forms of violence.

Ethical and Strategic Approaches to NVA

There are, broadly speaking, two schools of thought about how NVA ought to be utilized: the ethical view advanced most popularly by Mohandas Gandhi and Martin Luther King, Jr., and the strategic or pragmatic view advanced most popularly by Gene Sharp. Understanding these two schools of thought will help gain a more thorough appreciation of what NVA is by examining their goals and objectives. After looking at these two approaches, we will look more closely at the techniques employed to understand how NVA works, why it is effective, and how we can teach these techniques to promote a stronger participatory and emancipatory democracy to oppose right-wing extremist policies that threaten our rights and freedoms.

It is important to note that there is nothing in the methods of nonviolence that preclude it from being used for harmful purposes. Richard Spencer, for example, uses symbolic methods of NVA when giving his racist speeches on college campuses as a means of persuading people to stand up in defense of white supremacy. Trump also uses it to whip up support for his hateful policies against immigrants. To combat these negative uses of NVA, many advocate for a principled or ethical approach.

Principled approaches, in theory, focus on transforming activists and the opposition into more ethical persons who seek the love, truth, and connectedness of all living beings. This is both its strength and weakness; while it guides people into working for justice without the use of violence, coercion, or punishing methods, it demands a level of sacrifice from its followers that not all are willing to give. Additionally, its goal of changing opponents into loving and just beings is not realistic in many cases.

Ethical Approach

For Gandhi and King, NVA was a way for activists to awaken and live out the spiritual ideals of truth and goodness. It was also a way to awaken these ideals in one's opponents. Gandhi's *satyagraha*, [11] which literally means "truth-force" or "soul-force" is a process of helping to bring about an "awakened" public that sees what is right, true, and just. [12] It is based on the Hindu view that all people are part of one reality, and to harm another is to harm the one true self. Coercive, punitive, or humiliating practices are seen as counterproductive because they obstruct the development of loving connectedness as a way of life. The purpose of *satyagraha* is to turn the ethical ideals of Hinduism into practice by working toward social justice. For Gandhi, then, nonviolent action was a way to bring about a spiritual transformation in his followers and adversaries.

Martin Luther King, Jr. also sought to arouse the spirit of love through the practice of nonviolence. His ethics are drawn from Christian teachings, but he shared Gandhi's goal of personal transformation for both activists and opponents. A*gape*, connection and love to all sentient beings, was a fundamental guide for King. [13] It encourages activists to accept their own suffering from their foes' reprisals rather than inflicting it onto others. This redeems the spirit of the activist through its selflessness and directs the energy of resistance towards corrupt systems and organizations rather than particular individuals.

Gandhi and King were not averse to making conditions so impossible for their opponents that they had little choice but to give in to the demands of the resistance. Yet, their methods were not devised to degrade, humiliate, or in any other way emotionally coerce the opposition into accepting the demands of the activists. Rather, their goal was to awaken in their rivals the love toward all beings. Such change is not only systemic and structural; it is spiritual where people learn to invite love and understanding into their hearts.

For both Gandhi and King, the means to achieving justice are as important as the ends. If we are fighting for equal pay for equal work, and we achieve this by threatening employers with violence should they not cooperate, we will have equal pay for a while, but we will also have a wary and plotting enemy. On the other hand, if we receive equal pay through ethical nonviolent and noncoercive means, we will have transformed the beliefs and values of our employers, at least to some degree and, thus, we not only have a fair wage, we have a better relationship with our employers. If we attain what we want through unethical endeavors, we not only jeopardize just relations with others, we risk harming our moral selves and creating a society in which the ends justify the means.

The goal of ethical nonviolence, then, is not to harm the opponent or strong-arm them into submission. Rather, the goal is to transform them into recognizing the power of love so people become more spiritually connected. This is not as idealistic as it may sound. Neither Gandhi nor King believed that kind words and spiritual teachings would persuade their rivals. Instead, they believed that people in positions of authority will come to respect the courage of those who go up against them knowing they are likely to be beaten, jailed, and possibly killed. Gandhi and King believed that, eventually, enough rulers will come to believe their contested policies are wrong when they see the impact they have on activists who magnify them. People change when they witness protesters' willingness to accept the hostile and violent reprisals without backing down or responding with violence. Such moral strength affects people deeply; it can be transformative.

Gandhi's and King's transformational approach is its major strength because it makes society more ethical and it prevents people from using NVA for immoral and unjust causes. White supremacists, for example, would violate the ethical standards of principled approaches to NVA when marching in support of racist laws. In adopting principled approaches to NVA, we ensure that only those seeking to develop social justice can properly call what they are doing NVA.

One major weakness of principled nonviolence is it requires individuals or, perhaps more importantly, entire groups and populations to buy into the ethical principles guiding the action. Gandhi required "utter selflessness"[14] of practitioners of nonviolent noncooperation: "He who has not learnt to sacrifice his property and even his family when necessary can never non-co-operate."[15] This normative view asks a great deal of people and it can, therefore, alienate many who are not willing to sacrifice so much.

In multicultural nations, people have different and

sometimes even conflicting views on what constitutes worthy moral and ethical goals. Asking people to accept Gandhi's notion that nonviolence requires significant self-sacrifice in terms of property and family ties is quite foreign to most Westerners who do not view all sentient beings as part of the One timeless reality. Nonviolent action campaigns, particularly those waged against governments, require the participation of a large portion of the civilian population.[16]

It can be difficult to get a diverse range of people to unite under a narrow set of ethical tenets or to draw upon faith in a higher being to provide them with the strength or rationale for resisting. This is the weakness of ethical approaches. In multicultural nations such as the US, it may be easier to get people to unite under a broadly inclusive political ideal. Thus, the strength of a pragmatic approach is that it can attract more participants.

Strategic Approach

Gene Sharp claimed that one's ethical views are independent of one's ability to engage successfully in NVA.[17] For him, nonviolent action is a useful means to a political end rather than an avenue for moral elevation. Having studied Gandhi, Sharp developed his pragmatic approach, sometimes referred to as a techniques, strategic, or tactical approach. It focused on the practical usefulness of Gandhi's nonviolent methods rather than the ethical ideals they promote. As Weber explains in his writings on Sharp and Gandhi, "Sharp makes it clear that he is much less interested in the extreme religious pacifist and moral arguments approach ... preferring instead a 'technique approach."[18] Regardless of one's religious or moral views, Sharp claimed that the use of nonviolent methods enables anyone to effectively oppose even violent and authoritarian rulers.

A people's movement that strategically withholds its obedience can successfully counter the power of any governor. A pragmatic approach to NVA does not argue that there are no legitimate moral reasons to reject violence. Nor does it claim that Gandhi and King were anything but extraordinarily effective in their nonviolent campaigns. On the contrary, Sharp's methods were largely borrowed from Gandhi because he recognized their power. What Sharp set out to do was not dismiss the moral claims of Gandhi and King as unimportant or insignificant. Rather, Sharp worked to develop a theory of nonviolent action that did not *require* a particular moral outlook on violence. The focus, for Sharp, was on the *effectiveness*, rather than the moral virtue or superiority, of nonviolent action.

A weakness of strategic approaches is that, although they can draw the support of entire populations of people with diverse ethical views, they can be used for unjust purposes. For example, it has been employed by the US Tea Party and Free-Staters to subvert progressive economic policies and environmental protections. It was also used by Russia to influence the 2016 US presidential election, by conservative extremist religious groups to reduce women's reproductive rights, and by white supremacists to enforce racist policies. In Warsaw in 2017, an estimated 60,000 people took to the streets to march for a "pure Poland," one where Jews and Muslims are not welcome.[19] When there are no ethical rules or ideals to guide nonviolent action, there is nothing precluding it from being used to degrade, oppress, and endanger others. The primary focus of pragmatic approaches is to effect change. The methods, therefore, are available to anyone for any purpose.

Although we do not want to constrain a nonviolent movement by imposing strict normative ideals that may alienate many who do not buy into them, we do need some way of ensuring that nonviolent action is used to promote such political ideals as social justice and economic, cultural, and political equality. If NVA is to help the Resistance more effectively promote justice and equity, we need to make sure it is defined in such a way that it cannot be used to pursue unprincipled goals, and at the same time, it is both broadly inclusive and effective.

A Participatory Process Approach to Nonviolent Action

One way to define NVA so it has all the benefits of the ethical approach and of the strategic approach but neither of their weaknesses is to define it in terms of educational theorist Ken Howe's *participatory ideal*.[20] While discussion of Howe's participatory ideal may seem a bit abstract or theoretical, I ask the reader to bear with me. I think it's important to understand Howe's notion because it is key in appreciating how NVA cannot only serve as an appropriate 3rd alternative to ethical and strategic approaches. It can also help one see how engaging in NVA restructures society in a way that promotes equal opportunity for all in the decision-making processes that help people reclaim their power.

Howe's participatory ideal is based on what political philosophers call a *liberal egalitarian* framework.[21] This can be understood by breaking down politically liberal views into Howe's three categories: formal, compensatory, and participatory. I give a brief description of each to show how the third category is conducive to promoting NVA.

Formalists argue that political equality is best achieved by removing any laws or policies that prevent individuals from gaining access to societal goods and resources. Howe claims that formal approaches to equality require "only the absence of formal barriers to participation based on morally irrelevant criteria such as race and gender."[22] Thus, legally sanctioned racial and sexual discrimination in the workplace would not be tolerated. Also, children with disabilities should not be prevented from attending schools along with their peers. This is all very good in so far as it goes but removing formal barriers does not address structural oppression or endemic poverty.

Consider two men: Carl and Stanley. Carl, a working-class father whose pay checks go entirely to feeding, housing, clothing, and educating his family, is legally allowed to purchase health insurance. Stanley was raised by wealthy parents, went to expensive prep schools, attended an elite university, and has a job where he makes over 300k/year plus bonuses. According to formalists, both Carl and Stanley are given an equal opportunity to receive health care. For formalists, systemic poverty or oppression plays no significant role in the fair or just differences in each person's ability to pursue their needs and goals. All that is required is that each individual be legally afforded an opportunity to do so. Formalists will concede that Carl is at a disadvantage but they would claim it is not an unfair disadvantage in that it was not caused by any particular unjust transaction that advantaged Stanley.

Compensatory interpretations of equality and liberty recognize that some individuals from certain groups are disadvantaged through no fault of their own and must therefore be given enough compensation to provide a more genuinely equal opportunity. In the example above, Carl would need to have access to subsidies that allow him to afford adequate insurance for him and his family. Medicaid, for example, is a compensatory program that provides working class and poor families access to health care. Compensatory programs make a difference in the lives of individuals. However, they do not necessarily alter unjust power structures.

Compensatory interpretations of equality are criticized from both the left and right ends of the political spectrum. On the right end, such as libertarians and conservatives, compensation is viewed as government interference in the private affairs of individuals and creates an unwanted dependency of such individuals on the aid of the government. On the left end, compensation is criticized for not doing enough to address the causes of marginalization and oppression.

The participatory view adopts formalist approaches of removing formal barriers against equality. Additionally, participatory theorists support compensatory programs such as Medicaid, Meals on Wheels, and Head Start to people who are at a distinct and unfair disadvantage. The participatory approach, however, as discussed by Howe, places primary focus on people from oppressed groups in society who have been largely left out of the decision-making and formulating processes in "designing the basic institutions of society."[23] Howe's participatory ideal interprets equality in terms of individuals' opportunity to participate in shaping societal structures that affect how people come to know themselves. It also defines equality in terms of what people believe about their own possible future goals, how they decide what choices are worth wanting, and the relationships people have with one another in terms of socio-economic and political power.

Whether or not individuals have equal opportunity "can be understood only within a context of choice, the features of which are determined by the interaction between individuals and social conditions."[24] Political scientist Tom Langford supports this view with his empirical study on union democracy. He writes that workers' participation is mistakenly measured by how many people take part in the various democratic processes. He argues that there is a false perception that the more people participate (say, 85% of union workers filled out a survey, attended a meeting, or voted), the more representative the decisions are. In the goal of consensus building, he found that with the unions he studied, the marginalized voices are sometimes silenced and the resulting consensus is falsely purported to represent the needs of all.[25]

Langford's study[26] illustrates a critical aspect of NVA: gaining a majority decision does not necessarily mean one acquires a decision that represents the needs of minority groups. As researcher Steven Corbett[27] found, who studied British civilian political participation, social empowerment derives from the ability of individuals to engage with others as equals in the various spheres of their lives. In enacting NVA, it is imperative that larger groups' voices do not drown out minority groups' needs.

The Participatory Approach and the Resistance

Howe's participatory ideal can help the Resistance become more powerful in the following ways.

1. Engaging in nonviolent action guided by the participatory ideal helps ensure not only the consent of the majority; it also requires that people from across the multicultural spectrum play a significant role in developing the rules, structures, narratives, and practices of newly formed governing systems. Such a multi-group approach means that no single collective, individual, or organization can engage in NVA for private gains or for oppressive and discriminatory purposes. The Women's March held on 21 January 2017 was the result of a collaborative effort by an ethnically diverse group of women to ensure that it did not only represent the needs of white women.

2. It draws on the advantages of strategic approaches' ability to include people from a wide range of ethical viewpoints while still requiring activists to operate in accordance with the

principles of equal opportunity. This encourages participants to build a society that works to meet the needs of everyone, and thus serves the interests of peace and justice.

3. It encourages individuals to learn about oppression so that choices are made from a place of understanding. This is what is now being referred to in the popular vernacular as "woke." For example, women, black and brown people make choices that benefit their lives better when they are "woke" to the oppression that exists against them in society.

4. In sum, taking the effectiveness of nonviolent action as a central focus, but regulating it so it can only be used for peaceful purposes, allows us to advocate for not just NVA, but NVA for peace (NVAp), an approach that blends what is best in both strategic and ethical methods of nonviolent action.

Chapter Three
Deconstructing Power

To fully appreciate how and why NVAp (Nonviolent Action for Peace) is effective, we need to understand how rulers maintain their power. First, it is important to recognize that power does not come from within anyone. Rather, it comes from one's external environment. Rulers depend upon what Gene Sharp referred to as "pillars" of support to provide them with and help them maintain their power. These pillars exist in society and allow rulers to be seen as authority figures, issue commands with confidence, and carry out tasks with efficiency.

Identifying these pillars helps us see what is required for any ruler to have power. It helps activists see what they need to undermine in order to redistribute power in society by shifting it away from corrupt rulers and into the hands of the people and more able, just leaders. When rulers lose the support given by these pillars, when they are increasingly isolated from them, they lose power.

Pillars of Support

In our democratic society, the most prominent pillars of support for our lawmakers are the following: public service, military, political party, labor organizations, material resources, public opinion, and allies. For rulers to issue commands and have them carried out, the rulers must be able to rely on the strength of these seven support systems. Without this support, rulers have no power. Taking each in turn, I first describe what they are to show how they supports a ruler's power. I follow that up by discussing how a NVAp movement can work to dismantle them in order to shift the power away from corrupt leaders and systems.

Public Service

Public service includes fire fighters, health care workers, law enforcement employees, transportation and roads workers, mail service personnel, social workers, parks and recreation employees, and so on. Every one of these professions helps keep society functioning by providing people with vital services. If any one of these groups stops functioning, society would be adversely impacted to a considerable degree. If they refused to cooperate with the demands of the rulers, the rulers would lose a significant amount of power. Imagine, for example, trying to command obedience from people without the cooperation of law enforcement. As another example, imagine if health care workers refused to comply with insurance policies set by government legislation. In a final example, imagine what might happen if public transportation employees went on strike in protest against a particular law or practice of the government. Our governors need the full compliance of public service employees to maintain their ability to hold power over the people.

One way to attack this pillar is to work toward getting public service employees on the side of the resistance. This can be done by continually advancing the message of the opposition's injustices through the engagement of peaceful protests such as letter writing campaigns to news outlets, flyers, social media posts, radio interviews, art displays, billboards, and public speeches. One of the great strengths of NVAp is that it is organized and carried out by average citizens who occupy a multitude of different professions. Many are civil servants and many others have friends and family who work in the public service sector. This association helps public service workers feel connected to the resistance. Additionally, it is fairly easy for public service workers to relate to the grievances of those in the resistance because they, like resisters, suffer from the same injustices and harms inflicted by the opposition.

State prosecutors can help by refusing to arraign resistance activists who commit minor offenses; police officers can show sympathy by dragging their feet and being very slow or refusing to break up peaceful protests; health care workers can treat resisters for free who were wounded during a peaceful protest; and educators can support student walkouts and engage in work-to-rule type actions. Put simply, public service workers serve the vital needs of the public. When their allegiance switches from the opposition or even from a neutral stance to join the resistance, the opposition loses a crucial area of cooperation needed to effectively maintain their authority.

Military

The military includes all officers, enlisted personnel, and support staff of every branch of the armed services. It is relatively easy to see how rulers require the cooperation of the military to maintain power. Foreign nations would no longer pay attention to the ruler's edicts, and international relations would favor those leaders who have the obedience of their military. In addition, massive resistance demonstrations within one's own country would not need to fear opposition from military policing. In resistance movements throughout history, when the military switches their allegiance away from the governors to the resistance, the governors are forced to step down because their ability to rule has entirely disintegrated.

As with civil servants, many who serve in the military are ordinary citizens who have a great deal in common with those in the resistance. In extreme cases where a people power movement is seeking to oust a government leader or an entire government, gaining the trust and loyalty of the military to the point where they will no longer serve the government, marks the end of the government's ability to rule. Yet, in less extreme cases, as when the people are looking to alter particular policies or certain elected members of a political party in a democratic system, winning the allegiance of the military can be just as important, but it may be less dramatic.

Imagine, for example, the military openly questioning the decisions of the government and expressing their disapproval of a government's stated position. The military can also fail to notice infractions the government is telling them they must respond to such as denying acceptance of transgender people. Furthermore, they can wear a protest symbol on their uniforms during a government mandated parade. These gestures of loyalty to the resistance and disapproval of the government are important indications that the government is losing their ability to command total obedience from the one area of the country on which they should be able to rely.

Political Party

Support from one's political party is also an essential aspect of maintaining power in this country. Our elected officials depend on their Party for financial support, a platform they can use to sell themselves to the public, and for cooperation in getting legislation passed. Without backing from one's Party, it is nearly impossible to get elected. Once elected, it's vital to hold on to the support of Party representatives in order to have the votes needed to get bills through the legislative process. Party members also help influence the media to project a positive image, which is necessary in order to uphold the people's approval. When Republicans started to turn away from Nixon, he found his power degenerating quickly. Additionally, when leading Democrats called on the resignation of Al Franken for sexual misconduct, Franken resigned.

Party officials can become convinced that they may lose in the upcoming election unless they take a stand against the major policies of their Party and in favor of those of the resistance. Additionally, if Party representatives come to believe that continuing to support their Party's leaders may mean a general loss of the public's trust, they may speak out and vote against their Party on disputed legislation. There does not need to be a total renunciation of a Party against those officials who are promoting unjust laws. Having some key members voice dissenting views about their Party's policies and voting against some legislation opposed by the resistance is enough to hurt the Party generally and the particular officials causing the most harm.

Labor Organizations
Labor organizations, such as unions and professional

associations, are vastly important in enabling any leader to rule. Without their cooperation, society would grind to a halt: vital jobs would not get done, services would not be offered, and the financial markets would take a serious hit. No person or group can rule over a society that is not working to accomplish necessary tasks. If the AFL-CIO called a workers' strike for some of their unions, rulers would see almost immediately how essential their cooperation is. For example, if the Communications Workers of America, the United Steelworkers, or the International Association of Machinists and Aerospace Workers decided to strike, there would be not only a breakdown in the normal functioning of a society, but also in a leader's ability to rule over that society. One's capacity to lead is gravely crippled if the workers who perform the necessary jobs of a society no longer obey the leader's edicts.

Although working class people are often most adversely affected by government greed and corruption, it is not always easy to get them to participate in a resistance movement whose primary focus is on political issues rather than on specific labor concerns. One reason is that they are often too busy working and raising families to take an active role in a resistance movement. Another reason is they cannot afford to risk losing wages or their jobs by engaging in labor strikes. If they work for the government, many don't want to take the chance that joining a politically controversial campaign may end in them being fired. Yet, with time, labor associations can be persuaded to join the movement.

When workers start to feel the harmful effects of the legislation being passed and realize it's only going to get worse, and when they see that the resistance movement is gaining strength, remaining peaceful, and fighting for laws that will benefit them, they will start to join the resistance. Even if labor organizations only participate in a one-day strike, it shows the government that they are organized enough to engage in a massive show of opposition. Often, actions taken by labor organizations have been the most important in a resistance movement because without labor, a society does not function. Also, when laborers strike, walk out, or engage in sick-outs, corporations that often fund politicians, lose a great deal of money.

Material Resources

Rulers need material resources to carry out necessary daily tasks. Consider the near to complete impossibility of running a society when a government does not have the resources required to produce food, materials for manufacturing goods, transportation to ship products, and so on. Also, consider how damaging to a governor's ability to lead if hundreds of thousands of citizens refused to pay their taxes or withheld them until certain elected officials resigned. Congress would have a very difficult time performing their duties if their meeting spaces were occupied by hundreds of people who refused to leave. And as a last example, imagine elected officials trying to pass laws or get re-elected without the financial contributions of donors.

This is just the tip of the iceberg. Our governors need material resources such as transportation vehicles, telephones, computers and other technological devices, workspaces, and even cleaning and office supplies. While some materials are fairly easy to access, others can be withheld from an organized resistance movement. Thus, it's important to keep in mind the necessity of material resources in supporting a ruler's ability to maintain power.

Blocking officials from gaining access to their workspaces is one fairly simple way to prevent leaders from having necessary material resources. Forming human chains in front of offices, conducting sit-ins within offices or in hallways to force people to walk over protesters to get into their workspaces, or spraying government buildings with harmless but noxious odors are some methods of taking away vital resources. Restricting the production of food and manufacturing is possible if laborers stopped working or companies shut down, but the costs to the public would far exceed those to the government.

Companies cannot simply refuse to ship goods to some without a very high risk of being sued or losing a significant amount of business. Thus, office resources and societal manufactured goods are not the best targets for attack in withdrawing material resources from governments. However, having functioning computers, printers, telephones, and other technology equipment is vital to any effective governance. Thus, people hired to maintain the technology could make repeated mistakes, enough to significantly reduce the efficiency of those who rely on them.

Public Opinion

Public opinion plays a critical role in a democracy for any leader to uphold their power. To enact policies, our governors need to convince people that the policies are for their benefit. This is why elected officials spend so much time, money, and effort in using the media to put the best spin on their policies and practices. To counter what he perceives as personal attacks by mainstream media outlets, Trump takes to the social media platform Twitter to post what he wants people to believe. Although the lies he tells on Twitter don't fool anyone but his ardent supporters, it does show how important public opinion is in legitimizing a ruler's authority.

Noam Chomsky argued that shaping public opinion is a principle concern in democratic governments' efforts to control the people.

Recognition that control of opinion is the foundation of government, from the most despotic to the most free, goes back at least to David Hume, but a qualification should be added. It is far more important in the more free societies, where obedience cannot be maintained by the lash. It is only natural that the modern institutions of thought control – frankly called propaganda before the word became unfashionable because of totalitarian associations – should have originated in the most free societies.[1]

Gaining positive media attention is paramount in allowing rulers to have a determining influence on what the public thinks about them, about the policies they are hoping to implement, and about the sort of society they want. If our leaders can shape what people believe our future should look like, they have tremendous power in instituting the sorts of changes they are seeking to make.

The best way to persuade the public to side with the resistance and not with the opposition is to remain nonviolent. Once a resistance uses violence, they are often viewed as fringe radicals with whom the public does not relate or sympathize. The public may also see violent resisters as being little better than the oppressive government they are trying to oppose. Remaining active but refusing to become violent often earns respect and admiration from the public, allowing the movement to grow.

The media plays a crucial role in swaying public opinion. If tens of thousands protest in the streets, it will have little impact if only a few people hear about it in the news. Resisters must be sure to publicize their actions widely by writing press releases, inviting people to film the events, and post write-ups, photos, and videos of the events everywhere on social media forums. One way to ensure the media will give an event a great deal of attention is if there promises to be an enormous number of participants. Another way to help ensure that the media publicizes the event is to indicate that the resisters' actions may cause hostile reactions or reprisals.

King noted that the power of civil disobedience was that it incited violent reactions from law enforcement, and this helped attract the media and earn sympathy for his movement. Civil disobedience, however, is not to be engaged in without serious planning; thus, it is not the first or always the best way to attract positive public attention. Remaining calm and peaceful while opposing unjust policies will persuade many in the public to side with the resistance over a government that continues to issue harmful and destructive laws.

Allies

A final major pillar of support in our society consists of close associates. Included in this are family, friends, aids, co-workers, employees, and loyal supporters. Trump is probably one of the best examples of how vital allies are to a leader holding onto power in a democracy. He has appointed family and what he believes are devoted friends in key White House positions to do the vast majority of the governing. Without their support, he would not be able to pursue his own agenda, which by all appearances is a self-aggrandizement campaign to improve the Trump brand. Additionally, Trump would have virtually no legitimacy among the people without his committed fans. With no close allies and associates, leaders do not have the psychological support they need to get through the daily rigors of their responsibilities nor do they have the advice and expert skills needed for the job.

Convincing allies to switch their allegiance is quite difficult. Typically, a leader's closest allies are people s/he has learned to trust because they are genuinely loyal. This is not always the case, however. There are times when people are close because it benefits them. If they come to see that they would profit more by separating from the leader, they can be persuaded to do so. Additionally, if the resistance can get allies to say or do something the leader would likely find disloyal, the leader may dismiss them, doing the work for the resistance of losing close associates. Quite often, however, allies are so committed to being loyal that putting energy into changing their views is a waste of time. Instead, it is best to oppose them with continual efforts to prove them wrong, model morally superior behavior, and build structures of people power that do not allow them the chance to continue their harmful practices.

If we picture the pillars of support as literal pillars upon which leaders must stand to have the authority to rule, we begin to see that the people must remove the pillars out from under the rulers and place them under new people and in a new formation that allows for a redistribution of power, one that is more equitably shared with the people. Attacking the pillars of support not only causes current leaders to fall; it also affords society an opportunity to shift the balance of power. In other words, it affords citizens the chance to alter decision-making systems so leaders are more accountable to the people. For today's Resistance to successfully take down Trump and right-wing extremists, they need to determine how to remove the pillars out from under them as well as those who are promoting Trumpist hate, elitism, greed, and environmental destruction. Then to build the sort of society the Resistance envisions, they must work to ensure that the people share a place with elected leaders at the top of the pillars.

Consent Theory of Power

Implicit in understanding the pillars of support is the recognition that their strength relies on the cooperation of the people: public servants, military personnel, laborers, political party members, and allies. At its most basic level, political power is dependent on the people's willingness to obey the rulers. Sharp, King, Gandhi, and many others (see Hannah Arendt[2] and Leo Tolstoy[3]) base their theories of political strength on what is called the *consent theory of power*.

When I taught Peace Studies at a local high school, I asked my students to imagine I gave them four hours of homework every night, and they opposed this by all or most of them refusing to do the work. Many students replied that I could simply fail them. I agreed, but then I asked what would happen to me if all my students failed. A light came on and they realized they have far more power than they had thought. So, what is power, I asked them. Is it not the ability of a ruler to get others to obey her? As the teacher in the classroom, isn't the amount of power I have dependent on my ability to get my students to obey my wishes? If no one does what I want him or her to then I wouldn't have any power. The consent theory, therefore, states that the amount of power a ruler has is contingent on the willingness of others to consent to the ruler's demands.

We see this refusing of consent in the notion of civil disobedience; it is a nonviolent tactic used to oppose a rule or policy. When Rosa Parks refused to comply with the bus policy of giving up her seat for white people, when patriots dumped tea into the Boston harbor in protest of the British tea tax, when followers of Gandhi gathered salt in protest against the British imposed salt tax, when Thoreau refused to pay his poll tax in defiance of the Mexican-American War and slavery, each person and group was displaying that rulers have only as much power as the people are willing to give them through their consent. Gandhi said that one "can govern us only so long as we remain the governed,"[4] and King argued that civil disobedience is one of the most powerful weapons against the authority of power holders. While it may seem simple to say that people have to merely disobey a ruler to take away his power, disobedience is not easy for most people. Societal structures and cultural conditions impact whether or not, why, and how people obey.

Why People Obey

Gene Sharp recognized that the choice to obey occurs within a cultural context of long held and strongly enforced norms, habits, ideals, and beliefs.[5] This gives rise to three major factors that influence whether or not or to what degree people will obey a ruler. One is the perceived legitimacy of the ruler. The second is the willingness of rulers to impose sanctions on those who violate their laws, and the third is the strength and integrity of the resistance movement. Each of these alone has a significant influence on whether or not, or to what degree, people obey.

Perceived Legitimacy of the Rulers

People tend to cooperate with leaders they feel have a rightful position of power over the laws and policies that shape how they live. Typically, people comply with the rule of law, in part, because they would rather live in a society where people follow the rules. They believe that, for the most part, laws protect them and thus they and their loved ones are better off in communities where everyone obeys the laws. Additionally, they obey because obedience itself, to one who occupies a position of established authority, is seen as a moral good. To have people even consider disobeying their leaders, they must come to see them as having broken trust with the populace or as no longer holding a rightful place of power over the people.

Over time, when a resistance movement successfully reveals that the government authorities are so corrupt that they no longer deserve the people's respect, more people will join the movement and oppose these governors. This occurred in Serbia. According to international relations scholar Adam Roberts and historian Timothy Ash, resistance movements evolved in Serbia from a relatively small number of people expressing opposition to Milosevic's increasingly authoritarian rule. In two years, it grew to a majority of people protesting every day in major cities. In 2000, resisters demanded that Milosevic accept defeat from the September 2000 elections. One month later, Milosevic stepped down, "conceding power to an alliance of democratic parties called 'Zajedno' (Together)."[6] Although Milosevic once had popular support, his leading the country into war, his initiation of the draft, and his nationalistic policies eventually turned more and more of his people away from him, even some within his own Socialist Party. Trying to hold onto power by refusing to admit defeat in the elections, massive protests showed that he no longer had any legitimate authority to rule.

Ability of Rulers to Impose Sanctions

Another factor that impacts how or if people obey is the availability of rulers to impose sanctions against resisters. In authoritarian regimes, sanctions can be quite harsh, including disappearances, torture, jail, and death. People are greatly affected by fear of punishment. When they know they are likely to suffer significant reprisals for disobedience, they tend to obey. Less severe governments may impose laws that restrict protests to a point where protesters have little room to develop a strong movement. For example, a government may outlaw gatherings of more than 50 people in public spaces for the purpose of a political rally. They may justify this by claiming that any group larger than 50 risks forming into an unruly and violent mob. Public speeches that voice dissent against the injustices of the government may also be ruled illegal because they incite hostility and violence. Violators can be heavily fined, subjected to high-pressure hoses or tear gas from police, and arrested and jailed.

More subtle, nevertheless very powerful methods of eliciting compliance is the ability of rulers to convince the people that obedience serves their best interests and shows an appropriate level of patriotism. When people don't obey, then they are to a degree shunned as being troublemakers and antipatriotic. Generally, the public does not want to hear or accept the views of such radicals, and they are quietly but definitely nudged into silence.

Regardless of how able and willing rulers are to impose sanctions, there are ways to get people to take action against rulers. The best way is to highlight the rulers' corruption and harmful practices. This can be done in two different ways. One way is to publish the rulers' actions and policies in leaflets, social media, letters to the editor, signs, speeches, theater, and music. Another way is to prod the leaders into responding to the resistance with hostility so as to display their brutality.

When powerful people use violence against peaceful protesters, the resistance gains the moral high ground; it earns sympathy and respect from the people for showing courage by refusing to back down while remaining nonviolent against a seemingly more powerful force. During the current people power movement in the Philippines, for example, Duterte is attempting to shut down his opposition by enforcing severe punishments against protesters. In December 2017, several protesters were executed. His brutality has had the opposite effect than he intended, however; the resistance groups have coalesced and grown stronger.[7]

Strength and Integrity of a Resistance Movement

The last factor Gene Sharp raised about what influences people's obedience is the strength and integrity of a rebel or resistance movement. Before people join a movement against a leader or group of leaders, three things must be present. The first thing is that people must see their living conditions as intolerable. Typically, this is when they are suffering economically, either from poor wages, high unemployment rates, rapidly increasing costs of living, and an out of control inflation rate. People also feel their living conditions are not tolerable when political conditions become too restrictive and oppressive, such as when they suffer severe reprisals for expressing their political views or experience extreme discrimination and hateful policies.

The second thing that must be present for people to join a resistance movement is seeing that a particular group of leaders is responsible for the people's living conditions. Because government officials are usually responsible for a society's economic and political quality of life, people may view them as the cause of their unendurable living conditions. When paired with a luxurious life of those in power who are impoverishing and oppressing the masses, the leaders can lose their legitimacy and the people are willing to rebel against them.

The third and final thing that must be present is a resistance needs to be viewed as a viable, realistic way of defeating the leaders. Sociologist Sharon Erikson Nepstad explains that the Tunisian Revolution was born in 2010 out of a feeling of anger from the increasing prices in food, poor living conditions for many Tunisians, high unemployment rates, political corruption, and restriction of political freedoms. The people saw the corrupt president Zine El Abidine Ben Ali as the major cause of the worsening conditions from which they were suffering. These conditions brought together students, laborers, and professionals who shared the goals of resisting the president's increasingly harsh policies.[8]

This diverse coalition of society's groups created a movement perceived as strong enough to take on Ben Ali, even to the point of violating his policies that restricted protests. In December 2010, hundreds of thousands of nonviolent resisters violated curfew to march in mass demonstrations. Labor unions, such as those for lawyers and teachers, engaged in nationwide strikes in January 2011. Despite Ben Ali's efforts to impose sanctions by shutting down the universities, the resistance did not back down. Ben Ali tried silencing protestors by making accommodations: he agreed to not go forward with his plan of making himself constitutionality allowed to remain president into perpetuity. Yet, the resistance never weakened. When the military switched their allegiance to the resistance in January, Ben Ali stepped down and fled to Saudi Arabia.

While disobedience of the masses undermines the power of rulers, it is not an easy thing to elicit due to the three factors discussed above: perceived legitimacy of the rulers, ability of rulers to impose sanctions, and the integrity of the resistance movement. Furthermore, mass disobedience requires a tremendous amount of strategic organization to get a substantial number of people working together in a unified action of opposition. Finally, disobedience comes with great risk of suffering significant costs. When workers strike, for example, they risk losing wages. Students who participate in a school walkout risk failing grades, expulsion, and losing college acceptances. When people violate the law, they risk being manhandled by law enforcement and jailed. These costs are often too great for most people; thus, attacking the power of rulers is not as simple as calling on the masses to disobey.

NVAp requires that the people engage in a wide variety of actions, not just disobedience, that are strategically planned to topple the pillars of support upon which the rulers depend for their authority. These actions can be categorized into four different groups, separated by the particular set of goals they are best at achieving, and they are discussed in detail in the next chapter. We will see that, while some actions are good at recruiting new members to the resistance, others directly threaten the ability of rulers to carry out their tasks.

Chapter Four
Techniques and Methods of NVAp

Gene Sharp's 198 Methods of Nonviolence

Gene Sharp identified what is now famously known as his 198 methods of nonviolent action.[1] He placed these methods under three general categories: protest and persuasion, non-cooperation, and intervention. I regroup them as a means of highlighting the impressive successes of today's Resistance and suggesting ways the Resistance can become even more effective. Sharp's categories are apt descriptions of the various methods of nonviolent action. I give a brief description of each then explain why I have chosen to re-categorize them into four groups.

Protest and persuasion methods, such as marches, letter writing, signs, and public speeches are all designed to express disapproval of certain policies and practices of leaders. They are also designed to persuade people of the appropriateness of the movement's goals and methods, so they join to make the movement stronger. Non-cooperation describes methods that show leaders the people are questioning whether they will cooperate with and obey the rulers' demands. Strikes, boycotts, work-to-rule, foot dragging, and sit-ins are examples of actions where people show an unwillingness to comply with the rules and structural practices that benefit the rulers. Intervention is a set of methods where people intervene or interfere in the rulers' abilities to carry out their tasks. Setting up alternative organizations, forming human chains, occupying government offices, and forming a people's interim government are all methods that make it very difficult for governors to continue the daily tasks needed to govern the people.

During the first year, the Resistance methods fell within Sharp's category, *protest and persuasion*:[2] marches, rallies, letter writing, and communicating with legislators. While the marches and rallies proved very effective in showing Trump and his cohorts that they had massive opposition, and they were successful in getting people to join the movement, they had only a minor impact on altering the dangerous and destructive policies coming out of the White House and Congress. What was far more effective was the work Resisters did in communicating with legislators. I wanted to separate these two different areas of work because they were and still are having very different impacts on our elected officials. Therefore, I break Sharp's protest and persuasion into two categories: *symbolic acts* and *political involvement*, which I discuss below.

Sharp's term "noncooperation"[3] was not resonating with those I spoke to in the Resistance because it sounded too radical, too akin to civil disobedience, which involved breaking laws and possibly, therefore, turning people off from the moral high ground the Resistance had achieved. Noncooperation, however, entails both legal and illegal methods. It also entails methods that comply with rules and those that do no. To make this distinction clearer, I created two separate categories: those that are *disruptive* or *coercive* but are legal and obey the rules, and those that are illegal or legally *noncompliant*. Because the methods in Sharp's category of "intervention" fall within both the *disruptive* category and the category of *noncompliance*, depending on what sort of disruption is enacted, I did not need to create a fifth category to encompass those methods. Thus, the four categories I devised are: symbolic resistance, political involvement, disruption and coercion, and noncompliance.

Symbolic Resistance

Symbolic resistance uses symbols or symbolic acts to display messages of resistance or opposition. Its purpose is twofold: to show the ruling powers that there is a movement against their policies, and to persuade bystanders and even members of the ruling elite to join the movement. Some examples include displaying symbols, words, or phrases on buttons, t-shirts, scarves, bumper stickers, posters, artwork, social media memes, and hash tag trends. By displaying symbols of the Resistance in today's society, we not only show that we support it, but we also provide a visual indication that the Resistance is active and present.

The more symbols displayed by individuals, businesses, and organizations, the stronger the message of the resistance's presence. NVAp (nonviolent action for peace) requires large numbers from diverse groups to be effective in opposing powerful rulers. One way to recruit new members and maintain existing members is to show that the movement is strong. While there may not be protests visible every day or even every week, symbols can serve the purpose of maintaining the energy of the resistance.

There are many historical examples of using symbols as a method of protest. Posting pictures of resistance leaders, such as those of Gandhi and Nehru for Indian independence and Svoboda and Dubcek for Czechoslovakian independence, was done to display the powerful leadership of the resistance.[4] 18th century French revolutionists wore the "red cap of liberty," and Danish students wore white and blue hats to protest the Nazi occupation.[5] The two fingered peace sign has been used frequently by anti-war protestors around the world, and the one fingered protest was used famously by a government employee as she was riding her bicycle past the Trump motorcade.

Symbolic protest can also take the form of labeling, signs, pamphlets, and public actions. With labeling, resistance members seek to shape the narrative of movements, cultural groups, historic events, and individual people. Some Mexican-Americans, for example, have taken up the label "Chicano" instead of "Hispanic" as a way of highlighting their native Nahuatl language over the language of the Spanish conquerors.[6] In the United States, black Americans have a history of re-naming themselves in defiance against white labels of degradation and inferiority.[7] The term "black" emphasizes that "black is beautiful," and "African-American" highlights their African roots.

Various forms of signage are also symbols. Such things as banners, bumper stickers, yard signs, billboards, hashtags, and even skywriting fit into this category. Much like hats, pictures, and other non-verbal symbols, signs represent the presence of the resistance but can add a level of explanation with the use of words. Thus, while a sign can just indicate the existence of opposition as in today's use of "Resist" bumper stickers, banners, memes, and hashtags such as "Protect our Health Care" provide a bit more clarity on what is being demanded or opposed.

Pamphlets and leaflets seek to give even more information about the views and needs of the resistance. Women suffragettes passed out leaflets to those attending a centennial celebration of the Declaration of Independence,[8] and during WWII pamphlets and leaflets were a main source of information used by resistance groups about Nazi cruelties.[9] Today, a primary source of resistance information is coming from social media posts and videos, blog posts, and letters to the editor.

Public actions can also be symbolic when their purpose is to illustrate a political point. Street theater, mock funerals, parades, dead-ins, marches, vigils, disrobings, and burnings are some examples. When the Yale women's rowing team's requests fell on deaf ears for equal facilities as the men, they marched across campus naked with Title IX painted on their bodies. Their point was that if women are primarily valued for their bodies, they would use them to get people's attention. Michael Moore used a mock funeral to demonstrate the cruelty of Humana insurance company's policies in his television show *The Awful Truth*.[10]

Today's Resistance is using red and white handmaid costumes based on Margaret Atwood's book *The Handmaid's Tale*[11] to send a message that current GOP attitudes and policies are oppressive to women. A more widespread and powerful symbolic act of the Resistance is the take-a-knee movement. This movement, started by Colin Kaepernick to oppose unfair treatment of African-Americans by law enforcement, caused tremendous media attention, especially after Trump's inflammatory comments about them being "sons-of-bitches."

Marches and vigils are the most popular form of symbolic protest. They were used extensively in European countries behind the Iron Curtain to oppose the rule of the Soviet Union.[12] In addition, thousands took to the streets in protest against Mubarak in Egypt, Milosevic in Serbia, Marcos of the Philippines, Britain in India, and in virtually every resistance movement of a nation against its government.

The Resistance movement has had some major and impressive successes using symbolic protest. The day after Trump's inauguration, the Woman's March that took place in cities and small towns throughout many countries in the world showed the Trump administration that millions of people were, at the very least, suspicious of his being able to lead the country in a positive direction. Most were downright critical and appalled that he won the election. The Science and Climate Marches that came months after were also massive, showing the GOP and Trump that the Resistance was strong. More recently, on March 24, 2018, Washington D.C. had its largest single day protest in US history with the March for Our Lives event.[13]

For marches and rallies and other symbolic forms of protest to show the opposition that the resistance is a threat, two important conditions must be met. First, they must be massive in size and made up of a diverse range of cultural and economic groups. Political scientist Erica Chenoweth and program director of nonviolent action at the US Institute of Peace Maria J. Stephan note from their research on the effectiveness of nonviolent versus violent campaigns that the two most important factors in a successful resistance movement have nothing to do with the type of government one is opposing, the rights and freedoms citizens have, or the degree of repression the government can and will use. Rather, it is the number and diversity of the resisters.

Chenoweth and Stephan claim that nonviolent fights are more successful than violent ones because they have a "participation advantage."[14] As they explain, both violent and nonviolent movements require a broad range of skills and resources as well as culturally diverse participation to provide the movement with all the knowledge and material needed to win. This diversity also illustrates the popularity of the campaign. Nonviolent campaigns are far more effective than violent ones in recruiting and maintaining these diverse, large numbers.

Violent campaigns are at a disadvantage for a few reasons. First, they cannot get the numbers and diversity of participants that nonviolent movements can. Second, the people see violent protestors as an extreme minority and not representing the people. Third, the government is far less willing to negotiate with violent resisters and unwilling to see their demands as legitimately representing the views of the people. Finally, the government is much better prepared and able to defeat an armed opponent than a large, diverse unarmed one organized to remove the pillars of authority upon which the rulers rely. A vital condition of any successful nonviolent resistance is to have a united, large, and diverse force.

The second condition that must be met for symbolic methods to be effective is that participants must behave in a more admirable, ethical manner than the opposition. Symbolic forms of nonviolent action are vital in helping grow the movement. Thus, it is essential that such tactics as marches and rallies can be used to illustrate their moral high ground. Most marches should be non-confrontational; they should engage a wide array of people, from families with children to older adults, displaying signs and chanting phrases of positive messages for change. In today's marches, "Love Trumps Hate," "Immigrants are Welcome Here," and "Save our Healthcare" are all examples.

As with any major conflict there needs to be tactical understandings and careful planning of different methods for different goals and situations. Thus, while most marches should be non-confrontational, some should incite hostile responses from the opposition. During King's Birmingham Campaign where he organized protests against "separate but equal" laws and other remnants of the South's Jim Crow laws, marchers set out to incite a reaction from their opposition and even sought to get arrested. Police used fire hoses and police dogs against men, women, and children. Many were arrested and the jails were filled over capacity.

As King stated in his famous Letter from a Birmingham Jail, "The purpose of ... direct action is to create a situation so crisis-packed that it will inevitably open the door to negotiation."[15] Turning high pressure hoses and sending police dogs against peacefully demonstrating men, women, older folks, and children helped demonstrate to the people the moral justness of the protestors' cause.

Harsh, repressive responses from governors meant to intimidate and impede resisters usually have the opposite effect. Similarly, when peaceful protests meet with hostile and especially violent reactions from civilians who support the governments' oppressive policies, the resistance earns sympathy and respect. Some who had not yet joined the movement will do so in order to oppose what they have come to see as a despicable foe. We saw this in today's Resistance when white supremacist James Alex Field, Jr. killed peaceful protestor Heather Hyer by running into her with his car. News agencies and social media posts were filled with outrage against such violence, as well they should, and even more generally, by such emboldened acts of racism. As a result, the Resistance gained strength and momentum in attacking the current administration's, at best, lax attitude against the horrific effects of white supremacy.

Knowing when a march or rally should be confrontational and when it should not requires careful planning based on an overall grand strategy. As Robert

Helvey says in the documentary "How to Start a Revolution," every large organization, particularly those with multiple moving parts, needs leaders.[16] Without them, one hand acts without the knowledge of what the other hand is doing and without an understanding of what the entire body wants to achieve or how it plans to reach its goals. This is why it's so important to teach NVAp to resisters because most people are unaware of how to develop as effective a movement as possible. Instead, different smaller groups learn through trial and error, often making costly mistakes.

A carefully planned, strategic campaign with strong leadership that comes from the resistance can help ensure that any given protest will have made as large an impact on the opposition as possible. Because the purposes of symbolic protest are to grow the movement and illustrate to the opposition how unpopular are their policies, developing coordinated actions that present a united front will achieve these goals far more than will a series of impromptu and disconnected actions. How this can be done for today's Resistance is explained in the next chapter.

Political Involvement

The second category of NVAp, political involvement, engages in displays of opposition by communicating with elected officials via mail, phone, or social media, by showing up at political hearings, supporting certain candidates, and running for office. The goal is twofold. First, it is to convince elected officials to support policies backed by the resistance and to contest those backed by the current administration. Second, political involvement seeks to demonstrate to political representatives that the resistance is watching them and will take action to oppose them if needed.

One of the largest networks of today's Resistance groups, Indivisible, was set up specifically for the purpose of "taking down Donald Trump's agenda."[17] Indivisible was started by two former congressional staffers. It is organized as a website that offers a guidebook on how groups throughout the country can effectively work against the current administration's policies. Indivisible claims to be using tactics employed by the Tea Party who successfully shifted "mainstream" Republicans much further right than they had been prior to Reagan. The primary tactics advocated by Indivisible are holding town meetings, visiting and calling officials' offices, writing emails and faxes to elected representatives, and filling the rooms of local and state political meetings to put pressure on their elected officials to reject the Trump and GOP policies.

Such tactics have made positive and significant differences in their use throughout history and in our current times. Today, people are flooding the phone lines of their elected representatives to put pressure on them to speak out and vote against the GOP's immigration ban, oppose the tax plan, protect the Affordable Care Act, fight against the US withdrawal from the Paris Climate agreement, and resist policies on de-regulating financial institutions, just to name a few. On a local level, in New Hampshire, where there are three Republicans and two Democrats on the Executive Council, Republican Councilman Russell Prescott was said to have admitted to changing his mind and voting to support Planned Parenthood because of all the people in his district who called his office.

Contacting local and national representatives have enjoyed some success. Democrats stood up against the GOP and enough Republicans pulled their support so that, in Trump's first year, several bills repeatedly failed to get the backing needed to pass. Political involvement is a very popular and effective method of NVAp for several reasons. One, it allows people from all walks of life to participate at a level they are comfortable. While some are more confident signing petitions, others choose to send faxes or make phone calls to representatives, and others prefer to occupy town halls and legislative hearing rooms to show their opposition to a proposed GOP policy. Because political involvement is typically legal in a democratic society, non-disruptive, and non-coercive, it is a safe and palatable way for most people to participate.

While this form of NVAp is particularly effective in

democratic societies and it has achieved some impressive wins for the Resistance, it cannot be relied upon as the sole or even primary method of change. The assumption behind today's political involvement methods seems to be that if Democrats replace Republicans in government, all our major problems will be solved. There is certainly some merit to this; Democrats in general do not support supply side economics, nor do they support the large-scale financial and corporate de-regulations advocated by our current GOP. As a group, they also have a better record on environmental protection policies, and they tend to appoint judicial positions to far more qualified and progressive people than the Trump administration is currently appointing.

Democrats, however, have been criticized for not doing nearly enough to institute policies for working class families, women, and people of color. For example, Doug Jones who defeated Republican Roy Moore by an impressive show of black women voters, declared within a week of his election that he will not join other Democratic senators in asking for Trump's resignation over sexual misconduct allegations. He claimed that the charges "are not new and he [Trump] was elected with those allegations at front and center."[18] While it may have been acceptable to not call for Trump's resignation because Jones believes all accusations should be thoroughly investigated before taking action, his reasons imply that Trump should remain

President even if the allegations are true because voters knew about his misconduct before voting. This does not seem to be a position that supports the women who voted him into office.

Joe Lieberman, who ran as a vice presidential candidate with Al Gore, was progressive on some issues, such as the environment. Yet he continued to be a staunch advocate of the Iraq War, and he was a strong supporter of big insurance and pharmaceutical companies, two industries that have a history of making it very difficult for working families to have affordable health care. Perhaps most blatantly of all, he endorsed John McCain over Barak Obama in the 2008 presidential elections.

The point here is not to promote some candidates or elected officials over others, but to show that electing Democrats, in and of itself, does not necessarily force the government to work for economic, cultural, and socio-political fairness and equity. An empowered people, organized and trained in NVAp, has a far better chance of ensuring that.

Disruption and Coercion

A third category of NVAp is Disruption and Coercion. These methods disrupt the administrations' ability to carry out their goals and tasks, and when enacted on a large-scale can coerce power holders into meeting protesters' demands. The purpose is to make it costlier for rulers to accomplish their goals and to see that the people have far more power than they initially thought or wanted to believe.

The primary difference between disruption and coercion is in degree. Disruption warns rulers that a more extreme movement could follow. While a limited, small-scale boycott, say of advertisers for Breitbart news website, can cause several companies to pull their ads from that site, it won't necessarily shut it down or stop all forms of extreme right-wing media programs. A much larger boycott, say of all advertisers of Breitbart, will likely shut down that site and will be a dire warning to other right-wing propaganda that they may be next. The larger the action, the more impact it has on the power elite. Thus, the same method can be either disruptive or coercive depending on the scale it takes. Put another way, a nonviolent action can either make it terribly inconvenient and costly for the power holders to continue with their practices or it can make it nearly impossible or extremely costly to do so.

Some methods in this category include: labor strikes, boycotts, sit-ins, human barricades, setting up alternative businesses, work-to-rule movements, sick-outs, foot dragging, foul odor occupations, and withdrawal of bank deposits. These methods are really where the rubber hits the pavement. Until a ruling body is disrupted in their efforts to enact their policies or coerced into changing them, they can largely ignore the protests against what they are doing. For example, although African-Americans and their allies protested against unfair segregation policies for years, it was not until the bus boycott in December of 1955 in Montgomery, Alabama that meaningful change occurred to end segregation in public spaces. After a year of boycotting the buses, the courts met all the demands of the NAACP when they ruled that the bus policy violated the 14th Amendment.[19]

The bus boycott is an interesting case to understand nonviolent action. Without going into too much detail, we see in this boycott some important characteristics of successful movements. Prior to this action, the NAACP worked through the courts to rule that the "separate but equal" reading of the 14th Amendment was inappropriate. The NAACP argued that segregation did not lead to equality, and thus the 14th Amendment was violated by segregation policies. A primary focus of their court efforts was in desegregating schools.[20]

In the 1954 Supreme Court ruling *Brown v. Board of Education*, along with several other cases challenging the separate but equal policies in education, blacks gained significantly toward equal educational opportunity. While this effort continues to this day, these court rulings certainly helped not only with desegregating schools, but desegregation policies in general. Yet there was still a great deal of work to do in gaining equal access and treatment in public spaces. The bus boycott was one of the earliest mass actions in the civil rights movement and it lead to the emergence of Martin Luther King, Jr. as a leader of the movement. Furthermore, because the vast majority of people who used the buses were African-Americans, boycotting it meant that alternatives for transportation had to be arranged. People organized carpooling, many walked, and black taxi-drivers reduced their prices for African-Americans to the price of bus fare.

King and other leaders also held regular meetings to sustain the energy and participation of the movement. Some of the key features of this successful campaign were leaders who spoke to the needs of the people and were strong and charismatic enough to inspire people to follow them, well-organized actions with clearly defined and articulated goals, and people trained and experienced in discussing their demands and negotiating with government rulers. The bus boycott was only one, albeit an historic, action in a long series taken on by civil rights activists for the end result of desegregating the buses. Its particular focus of altering bus policies was plainly defined as an integral part of a clearly expressed overall goal of acquiring equal rights for black Americans.

What we can learn from this boycott, as with many other nonviolent campaigns throughout history, is that NVAp cannot consist solely or even predominantly of symbolic and political involvement methods. Instead, a nonviolent campaign must more directly attack the pillars of the rulers' support. In today's Resistance, there has been a massive outcry against Fox News, and of Sean Hannity in particular, for their biased and sometimes even downright false reporting. Hashtag trends such as #FireHannity went viral on Twitter, but they did little to change Hannity's behavior. However, when Resisters called for a boycott in 2017 of Hannity's advertisers after Hannity supported Alabama Senate candidate Roy Moore—a man accused by several people of pedophilia—many of the advertisers pulled their ads, causing Hannity to withdraw his support of Moore.

Speaking out against a perceived injustice is important because it shows the rulers they are being opposed and it helps bring people into the resistance. However, it needs to be accompanied by more disruptive action, the kind that threatens the stability of the support upon which the rulers depend for their legitimacy, authority, and ability to conduct their business. Hannity and Fox News require advertisers. Without them, the show will not be funded. By threatening the source of their funding, Hannity altered his position.

Various actions of disruption and coercion have taken place throughout history. Two of the most common types of action are the economic boycott and the labor strike. In 1957, blacks in Alexandra, Johannesburg, South Africa protested the increase in fares by boycotting the buses. After twelve weeks and some sixty thousand participants, the boycott ended in victory for the protestors.[21] Looking at another example, the Solidarity movement of Poland in the 1970s began when the intelligentsia joined with workers by engaging in labor strikes to protest against trials of arrested workers and price increases.[22] A third example occurred in New England when Market Basket non-unionized workers participated in a successful strike to oppose the Board's firing of their boss, Arthur T. Demoulas, because the Board wanted more profits to go to shareholders rather than back into the business. Employees feared that if profits did not go back into the business, the store would risk being able to keep their prices low and maintain current employee wages and benefits.[23]

Disruptive and coercive methods of NVAp have more difficulty attracting large numbers of participants from diverse backgrounds because they are riskier than symbolic and political involvement methods. Yet once the rulers have lost to a significant degree their legitimacy, and the resistance movement acquires respect and sympathy from the people, disruptive and coercive methods can really undermine the pillars of authority. When a government is continuously being disrupted in their ability to carry out their agenda, and when it becomes extremely costly to do so, the resistance has gained tremendous success in shifting the balance of power away from that government and towards the people and more representative leaders.

Noncompliance

The fourth category of NVAp is noncompliance. These methods include a refusal to cooperate with and obey the orders, rules, and policies of power holders. While this may entail disruptive and coercive methods, it takes disruption and coercion to a further extreme, making it quite clear to rulers that they have lost the ability to elicit obedience from the people. Some examples include refusing to pay taxes, setting up alternative ruling bodies, forming alliances with foreign rulers, withdrawing from military service, noncompliance with law enforcement, and disobeying policies and laws.

There are several examples of nonviolent noncompliance in history; I name just a few to provide some illustration of the scale it can take on. In Nepal in 1990, resisters demanded the return of parliamentary democracy and constitutional monarchy. Although hundreds of peaceful protesters were injured and 50 died when government forces shot them, the protesters remained to demonstrate against the *panchayat* political system. Within a year, democratic elections took place.[24] Other examples include Russian secret police turning a blind eye to Jews settling in areas where it was illegal for them to live,[25] Iranian state workers refusing to run the propaganda programs issued by the Shah, several military supporters of James II of England switching their loyalties to William of

Orange in the Glorious Revolution, and American anti-war protesters during the Vietnam war burning their draft cards.

The Resistance engaged in nonviolent noncompliance after the Parkland, Florida shooting in February 2018 where Nikolas Cruz killed 17 people. From different high schools across the country, students walked out of school to put pressure on lawmakers to pass stricter gun legislation. In less than two weeks, they had a major impact on law makers and political candidates calling for gun reform. Some of the student survivors who were leading the protests received tremendous media coverage, which put pressure on elected officials to take some action. Trump proposed banning bump-stocks, and a leading GOP donor, Al Hoffman Jr. wrote an email to Republicans stating that he is withholding all donations until there is a ban on assault weapons.[26]

Withdrawing compliance not only makes it difficult to impossible for rulers to conduct necessary functions of society, it also reveals to the rulers that their power is entirely dependent on the people's compliance. This re-establishes the balance of power in favor of the people, yet it puts them at risk of receiving severe repressive responses. It also, however, puts them in the beneficial position of having their needs listened to and met. Engaging in noncompliance, therefore, comes with serious risks. However, if undertaken carefully and with thorough planning, the risks can be minimized. Also, if the resistance makes plans to address and respond to government repression, the risks can be minimized even more.

Powerful rulers do not give up their authority easily, and often resistance that truly threatens that authority will be met with harmful and destructive countermeasures. This is one reason why it's so important for activists engaging in noncompliance to be adequately trained in not only conducting the initial nonviolent action; they also must be trained in dealing appropriately with the possible reprisals.

Kinds of Changes

According to Gene Sharp,[27] there are four ways that a resistance can achieve victory: conversion, accommodation, coercion, and disintegration. I discuss each because it is important to understand that change does not always occur as a result of convincing the opposing side that they must alter their ways. Indeed, most often resistance movements produce change through force; that is, they give the opposition little to no alternative but to meet the demands of the resistance. It is also important to understand that voting people out is only one way of forcing change in a democracy. Furthermore, voting in new people does not improve corrupt structures that allow leaders to enact selfish and harmful laws. There are several other ways to institute change, most importantly, attacking the pillars of support upon which the governors rest their authority.

<u>Conversion</u>

The ideal form of success is conversion. This occurs when the opposition changes their views to adopt those of the resistance. The opposition comes to believe that what the resistance is advocating for is right and good. This sort of success is unusual, but it does occur. Gandhi and King sought conversion; they hoped nonviolent action would engender a transformative experience in practitioners and their opponents by opening their minds and their hearts to the love and interconnectedness of all sentient beings. This may seem an overly idealistic goal, yet it did have impressive successes.

When a ruling group sees protesters show incredible courage in their willingness to suffer and stand up nonviolently against armed opponents who are able to jail, torture, and even kill them, more than a few develop a respect for the protesters. Some even convert to their way of thinking. It is a remarkable thing to witness people able to receive blow after blow of their opponents' physical attacks and never raise a hand in retaliation, but also refuse to back down. This sort of experience changes people; it is for many, as Gandhi and King hoped, a transformative experience.

Unfortunately, it may be too much to expect that all or

even most power holders will come to adopt the views of those who challenge their power. Most often, people who stand to lose a great deal of authority will fight to the end to hold on to what they have. In most cases, then, conversion happens to bystanders who are initially unsure that the claims made by the resistance are accurate. They eventually come to believe that things are as bad as the resistance claims and that they are worth fighting against. In the current movement, many joined the Resistance when they became convinced that Trump and the right-wing GOP were jeopardizing our fundamental democratic rights and freedoms. People joined the movement because of the government's policies on immigration, women's reproductive rights, health care, gun laws, and taxes, as well as Trump's egregious comments that have emboldened white supremacists and Nazi sympathizers.

Conversion can also occur among important supporters of the opposition. In the Filipino People Power Movement and in the Serbian movement to unseat Milosevic, the resistance won over the loyalty of the military by changing their hearts and minds. During the US involvement in the Vietnam War, more and more of Nixon's supporters turned against him to side with the anti-war protestors. In today's Resistance, there has been little conversion among the GOP; yet some, such as Senator Jeff Flake, claim they are resigning because they can no longer be a part of what the Republican Party is becoming, and some are voting to support their constituents' wants rather than voting along party lines.

Accommodation

When protestors demand the types of changes that don't require governors to make any fundamental alterations to their policies, the governors can often accommodate the resistance. This can be done to appease some of the resisters' anger by convincing them that they are getting at least some of what they want. It can also be done to make it appear as if they are being fair by compromising with the resistance. While this benefits the resistance by giving them a little of what they ask for, it does not always significantly alter the power relations.

Trump's proposal to ban bump-stocks is an example of accommodation because it does a little to impose stricter gun laws but it does not pose a threat to the NRA selling all their other weapons including assault styled automatic and semi-automatic guns. Accommodation can be likened to releasing the relief valve on a steam turbine; it lets out a minor amount of pressure to avoid an explosion, but it does not alter the structure, which is necessary to resolve the problem. While accommodations do not always meet a protest movement's objectives, they are sometimes worth attaining as stepping-stones toward fully meeting those objectives. Banning bump-stocks is a good thing, but it is only one small step in reaching the objective of banning all assault weapons and large capacity ammunition feeders.

Accommodation can sometimes be more than just a release. It can also provide protesters with the fulfillment of their objectives. Governors may accommodate resisters if doing so does not jeopardize what rulers feel is more important. When American colonists fought against what they perceived as unfair taxation on paper goods, the British accommodated by repealing the Stamp Act in an effort to appease the colonists' growing rebellion. Thus, the colonists fulfilled their objective on getting rid of unfair taxes on paper goods.

In today's Resistance, there doesn't seem to have been any accommodations made that have fully met the goals of the Resistance. Initially, it appeared that the GOP made concessions to keep the ACA. Yet, they did this so they could get the votes needed to pass their overall tax bill with significant benefits for the wealthy and cuts to programs such as the ACA that protect working class and other vulnerable populations. From this, we see that accommodation can be a type of compromise which, although a good thing in some cases, in other cases is not. When the resisters lose something they are willing to give up in order to gain their objective, then the compromise is worthwhile. If, however, they must give up something of equal or more value than what they have gained, then accommodation is unacceptable.

Making changes through accommodation lies between

those made from conversion and coercion. When leaders accommodate, they do not alter their beliefs about what is right or ought to be the case, nor are they left without any reasonable alternative but to concede the resisters' demands. Instead, accommodation occurs when the rulers think they will benefit more by giving a little. Resisters can use this to their advantage by showing their opponents what they stand to gain by giving in. For example, activists can make their opponents see that the nonviolent movement will become significantly stronger unless the opponents make concessions. Although the opponents could still refuse to give in at all, they may decide it's in their best interests to make accommodations so they do not end up in a situation where they are left with little to no choice in the matter. Unlike coercion, accommodation is given when leaders still have some reasonable choice to act or not.

Coercion

Many believe that protesters can only succeed if they can *convince* their opponents to give in to their demands. This is not true. The power of nonviolent action gives protesters the tools and knowledge they need to *force* opponents to meet their demands. Resisters can coerce rulers to concede if they successfully shift the pillars of support out from under the rulers and place them under new leaders and the people. No government can continue to hold power if the people who enable society to function on a daily basis switch their allegiance towards new rulers within a new system that is more accountable to the people. This shift in loyalty results from targeting and attacking the pillars of support, and to do this, resisters must address people's tendency to obey.

People either obey or disobey based on three main criteria, as discussed in the chapter on Understanding Power:

    a. perceived legitimacy of the rulers,
    b. an ability of rulers to impose sanctions on violators of the law, and
    c. the relative strength of the resistance movement.

Today's Resisters must look to address these criteria so people will be willing to engage in strategic noncooperation with Trump and his supporters. Although many may not like or agree with a particular president or representative, they obey anyway out of respect for the position of authority s/he holds.

Even some who are serious critics of Trump feel he ought to be obeyed because he holds the title of Commander-in-Chief. Before a resistance movement seeks to withhold cooperation of the people, they must first delegitimize the authority of the rulers. Otherwise, the people can turn against the resistance as dangerous rebels. Additionally, a resistance movement must be organized enough to achieve a significant degree of success with acts of mass disobedience or their failure will weaken the legitimacy of the resistance and strengthen that of the rulers.

For coercion to be effective, a resistance movement must be sufficiently organized to carry out mass demonstrations, disruptive and coercive actions, and sustained, well-planned out methods of noncompliance and disobedience. The resistance must show that their opponents do not hold their positions of authority legitimately. In the case of today's Resistance, Trump and many he appointed in top positions are rapidly losing their legitimacy. This is happening in large part because of Trump's public buffoonery and hateful actions. It is also happening due to Mueller's increasing level of indictments based on a growing amount of very damaging information about Trump's financial dealings, his apparent acts of obstructing justice, and his close association with Russia in connection with not only his finances but with his presidential election.

The GOP is also losing their legitimacy by their stubborn refusal to act in accordance with the overwhelming expressed interests of their constituents concerning health care, gun legislation, environmental protection, immigration, and an economic policy that serves the needs of working classes. The Resistance is proving its own worth by remaining nonviolent and standing in support of what most Americans want: an effort to unite a divided nation by protecting the interests of all its people. Once the legitimacy of the opposition is sufficiently called into question, coercion may take place with an organized movement of strategic noncompliance, where the people switch their allegiance from the governors to the resistance.

It's important to note that when leaders begin to lose legitimacy they will fight back. Some will use force to silence the resisters. Some will manipulate the media to try and convince the people to side with them. And some who cannot control enough of the mainstream media, like Trump, will seek to discredit the media in hopes that the people will not believe any criticisms they have of him. Calling all news stories and media outlets who publish critical stories about Trump as "fake" is Trump's attempt to convince people to accept Trump's own version of events over those of such media giants as the *New York Times*, *Washington Post*, and CNN.

When this occurs, the task of Resisters is to continue to get their side of the story out into the public. Resistance leaders and participants need to be sure to publish their truths by getting coverage of their events, posting stories on social media, writing opinion articles in mainstream media, and posting evidence-based facts from respected organizations. In democracies such as ours, Trump does not control the media. Thus, it's important for the Resistance to keep getting the facts out to the public in a continuous effort to chip away at Trump's legitimacy.

Once Trump and the GOP lose the allegiance and cooperation of major sectors of society, they will be forced to either alter their policies or step down. Our government cannot lead if people refuse to follow. Organized, strategic noncompliance can coerce rulers to change or leave.

Disintegration

Typically, disintegration occurs in dictatorships or other authoritarian style governments. Whereas coercion can force some leaders to step down while allowing others to take their place without destroying the government or even the political party, disintegration involves a total collapse of an entire political party or even of an entire governmental system. One example of disintegration comes from the German people who completely disempowered the Kapp-Lüttwitz Putsch conservative rebel government after they successfully overthrew the legitimate Weimer Republic government in Berlin.

After only a few days of Germans engaging in massive general workers' strikes, the Kapp-Lüttwitz nationalist group was forced to leave.

> The general strike and political noncooperation
> made it impossible for the usurpers to govern,
> despite their successful occupation of Berlin. They

117

were unable to win the assistance of those persons and groups whose help was essential. Without that assistance and the submission of the people, the Kappists remained an impotent group, pretending to govern a country whose loyalty and support were reserved for the legal government. The *Putsch* therefore simply collapsed.[28]

The entire nationalist movement in Germany dissolved with the people's movement. While coercion would have forced certain Kappist leaders to step down, disintegration caused a complete shut-down of the entire Kappist group. Unlike authoritarian regimes, however, democracies are set up to allow for significant changes in leadership and policies without having a collapse of an entire party or governing system.

Democracies don't typically suffer disintegrations; yet today's Republican Party may be in danger of dissolving. The majority of Republicans are staying loyal to not only Trump himself but his policies, even as they appear to a growing number of Americans as misogynistic, racist, ethnically and religiously intolerant, xenophobic, hateful towards members of LGBTQ, and dangerous to the environment. This Trumpism is growing, even if Trump himself may eventually be defeated. As upholders of Trumpism, Republicans may lose the allegiance of the people. But that will not happen without a long, sustained, and organized nonviolent fight.

Furthermore, young people are polling as predominantly liberal and progressive and, if the polls are accurate and the trend continues, the Republicans will be facing possible extinction in the not-so-distant future. This is all conjecture, but it *does* reveal the marked difference between disintegration and coercion. The former is far more destructive, and it is not typically seen in democracies.

Today's Resistance, then, should not concern itself with the dissolution of any political party. Rather, they should stay focused on getting rid of those leaders, such as Trump and many of the GOP, as well as all other power holders who have shown time and again that they are harmful to democracy and the majority of the American people. They should also focus on developing relations of power that give the people a much stronger voice in the decision-making processes that shape our cultural practices and attitudes as well as our political policies.

Chapter Five
The Importance of Strategic Planning, Leadership, and Training in Today's Resistance

This chapter takes the information given in the previous chapters and applies it to today's Resistance. The aim is to provide practical suggestions on what the Resistance can do to move forward, become more powerful, and achieve success. The first order of business for the Resistance is to try and stem the flow of damaging policies being issued. The second task is to elect more progressive candidates that will support the fundamental goals and values of the Resistance. Finally, the Resistance needs to restructure our decisional processes so the people are more empowered to hold elected officials accountable.

What follows is an examination of essential features of an effective NVAp (nonviolent action for peace) movement including strategic plans with overall goals, individual campaigns with clearly stated objectives, and training and education of leaders and activists. These are all essential aspects of a resistance for it to effectively dismantle the pillars of support upon which Trump and his right-wing compatriots rely. The goal is to help the Resistance topple Trump's authority, dismantle the power of his impact in the future, and build structures that empower the people.

Strategic Planning

Success in any long-term endeavor, particularly those that involve large numbers of people and complex goals, requires leadership and detailed strategic planning. Without such planning, the endeavor is likely to fail. Consider, for example, a violent war. Imagine the US trying to win without a prudently mapped-out plan that serves as a guide in the continual strategizing of battles. Each battle is designed to meet certain objectives, and the objectives are formed to achieve an overall set of goals. Contingencies are developed for a wide variety of possible upsets, alterations in situations, and unexpected counter attacks.

Wars are carefully planned and organized events with educated and experienced leaders and well-trained soldiers who use a wide range of weapons. No one would even think to win a war without meeting these critical criteria. This is not to say that well-planned wars will always be successful. It is simply to point out that no war can hope to be successful without being thoroughly planned. Similarly, we cannot hope to have a successful nonviolent people power movement without strong and knowledgeable leaders and a grand strategy for planning individual campaigns consisting of hundreds of different nonviolent actions.

While passionate energy and dedicated commitment are important to engage activists in protests, it alone cannot bring about success. Gene Sharp argued that to oppose a governing group of people vested with the authority of their political offices and supported by tremendous wealth and power, a resistance needs far more than an avowed passion and call for change.

> Some people naively think that if they simply assert their goal strongly and firmly enough, long enough, it will somehow come to pass. Others assume that if they remain true to their principles and ideals and witness them in the face of adversity, then they are doing all they can to help to achieve them. Assertion of desirable goals and remaining loyal to ideals are admirable, but are in themselves grossly inadequate to change the status quo and bring into being designated goals.[1]

As with any goal in one's life, planning greatly increases the likelihood that one will achieve that goal. Strength in commitment and positive attitude is definitely helpful, but it is not enough. Sharp's writings show us that successful nonviolent movements are organized; they have leaders who articulate the people's clear goals, develop overall strategies, and plan campaigns involving multitudes of actions that help the people move toward their goals. Proper planning helps ensure that a movement maintains its momentum throughout the periods of little to no success and during times of internal struggles over strategies and tactics.

Momentum is aided by a movement being organized enough to motivate and marshal the disparate forces to act as a unified whole. For example, if there was a national campaign where hundreds of people in each voting district rallied in front of their delegates' offices, the media coverage would not be simply: *Hundreds of people protested today at the office of Senator Smith*. Instead, the media would be, *Hundreds of thousands of people showed up at their representatives' offices around the country in opposition to the proposed legislation.* Coordinated national campaigns, even when enacted in smaller, local areas, have a much greater impact than independently run actions.

Even if resisters in every state protested against the GOP tax bill, unless they all did so on the same day, it wouldn't carry the same weight. Representatives in each state could simply see local protest as fringe opposition. If, instead, they see the protestors in their state acting in unison with a planned national campaign, they will be far more responsive because they recognize that they are not just opposing a few hundred people. Rather, they are up against a unified coalition of groups working together as one. Thus,

123

to be more effective, enough to take down Trump and the GOP and to oppose Trump's impact in the future due to its rising strength, today's Resistance needs to become nationally organized. There must be an overall set of goals and a grand strategy to achieve these goals. There should also be smaller objectives, a wide range of campaigns to achieve the objectives, and hundreds of different methods to carry out the campaigns.

An important aspect of organizing a nonviolent movement is recognizing that plans and objectives are not created at one point in time then followed throughout the movement. That is not how a mass movement works. Once the overall goals are articulated and initial objectives and campaigns are created and carried out, new objectives and campaigns are best designed after seeing the impact of those that preceded them. The grand strategy, then, is not a recipe of planned actions, one after the other, to be followed from beginning to end. Rather, it is an overarching set of goals that help guide the continual creation of objectives, campaigns, and actions.

Leadership

National leadership in a resistance can help turn a series of smaller, ad hoc actions into a cohesive movement. In the struggle against Marcos, Cory Aquino was the leader, MLK lead the civil rights movement in the US, and Gandhi lead the campaign for Indian independence. These were single leaders who were remarkably charismatic and able organizers. Yet, individual leaders are not necessary. In the anti-Vietnam War movement, for example, instead of one person leading the campaign to end the war, there were a few major groups that protesters looked to for guidance. The Students for a Democratic Society (SDS) was one such group, the War Resistors League (WRL) was another, and Vietnam Veterans Against the War (VVAW) was another.

An individual leader has the advantage of rallying the masses through her/his dynamic personality. Yet, a group (or a few groups) has the advantage of better representing the diversity of their followers. As we saw with the 2017 Women's March, women from diverse cultural backgrounds were far better able to represent the voices of all women. When leaders come from different cultural groups and from a variety of organizations that deal with an array of issues, they are more able to represent the interests of the diverse views of resisters.

Leaders have various responsibilities. They must guide the development of the movement's overall goals, objectives, campaigns, and actions. It is their job to assess the goals to ascertain whether they are achievable within a reasonable timeframe. In addition, they need to determine what resources are necessary to carry out the campaigns. Leaders also have to help formulate contingency plans at a moment's notice because things can change so quickly in a resistance movement. If transportation workers are getting fired for going on strike, for example, a contingency plan may be to boycott all companies who fired their workers for participating in the strike. Finally, leaders work effectively with expert negotiators who seek to arrive at a solution acceptable to the two parties.

At the time of the writing of this book, there are so many groups, even national groups, trying to involve Resisters in a wide range of actions that it is difficult for Resisters to coalesce and form a unified movement. For example, there is: MoveOn, #GrabYourWallet, Our Revolution, Indivisible, ACLU, Justice Democrats, Tom Steyer Impeachment movement, Veterans United Against Trump, just to name a few. And Twitter is filled with Resisters calling on people to join mass actions such as boycotting Trump's 2018 State of the Union Address, engaging in workers' strikes, and marching on Washington DC to call for impeachment. All these groups and actions are necessary. The problem, however, is that there are too many groups vying for everyone's attention. The result is that the people's attention is divided rather than amassed into a single powerful movement.

The 2017 Women's March, the largest single-day protest march in US history, was an impressive display to our government that the opposition to Trump is enormous. Also, it helped launch thousands of individual Resistance groups throughout the country. However, it failed to utilize this momentum to build a national movement. Earlier in our history, during the US anti-Vietnam war movement, protesters came from a variety of factions, such as the black and Chicano civil rights, women's equality, labor unions, and anti-war groups. Yet, those different groups had more visible and unifying leadership than we have today.

Our current Resistance is fractured into far more and smaller groups with no centralized facilitators. What we lack today are organizing strategies and procedures for setting and achieving broadly articulated goals; thus, massive numbers are not showing up to protests often enough. With the advent of social media, there is a greater ability to communicate messages quickly over an enormous geographical area. However, because communication is so readily available, people are being inundated with hundreds, sometimes even thousands, of different messages every day and their attention is pulled in too many directions to focus on a unified call to action.

There is one group of people who has gained national attention and acquired the following of not only Resistance members, it has also attracted followers from outside the Resistance. The Parkland, Florida students who started the Never Again movement to end gun violence in schools and across the country has garnered the largest following since the Resistance began. People from a wide spectrum of political ideologies have come together in solidarity to promote common sense gun laws such as enforced background checks, and banning bump stocks, military grade weapons, and large capacity ammunition feeders. Although initially the focus of the Never Again movement was entirely on gun reform, this group of teens have provided the Resistance with something they haven't yet developed: dynamic, strong, organized, national leadership.

Leadership is essential to developing a movement that can rally a massive united force against Trump and his supporters at both the national and state levels. For nonviolent action campaigns to be effective, they must be large, diverse, and organized. Government leaders need to be confronted with the fact that their opposition is a powerful, united force that will not back down until their demands are met. Doing this requires national and state leaders who are skilled in organizing and maintaining momentum in massive movements and who are trained and educated in nonviolent action.

How to Form Effective and Representative Leadership

Perhaps the ideal leadership at the national level would be a group consisting of members of various prominent Resistance organizations that represent the different goals and values of the Resistance. Consider, for example, the Parkland teens working with the following groups: NARAL (women's reproductive rights), Black Lives Matter (civil rights and equal treatment by law enforcement for African-

Americans), Americas Voice (immigration rights in the U.S.), 350.org (environmental protection and sustainable practices), Moms Demand Action (advocates for reasonable gun safety laws), Human Right's Campaign (LGBTQ rights and safety), and Poor People's Campaign (economic justice for all oppressed persons). If the Resistance formed a multicultural leadership coalition consisting of members from each of these or similar groups, we would have leaders who speak to the major areas of concern for the Resistance. Organizations such as MoveOn, Indivisible, facilitators for the Women's March, and the originators of the #MeToo movement, all of whom already have an enormous following, could help support this new leadership. They could communicate the various objectives of the movement and rally their followers to join in nationwide campaigns.

In addition to having national leadership, each state should have its own leaders. Some changes that need to occur are at the state rather than national level. Laws on taxes, voting, education, marriage, driving, alcohol sales and consumption, and many more differ from one state to the next. And, just as is the case for national protests, state governors would be far more impacted by a massive statewide action than smaller, fragmented actions.

Like the national leadership, state leadership needs to be equally diverse both in their cultural makeup as well as their representation of the various issues concerning the Resistance. Some of the larger states may need more than a single leadership group; they may need three to four representing different geographical areas who themselves look to the state's leaders. Thus, while many New England states may only require one set of leaders each, California and Texas may need three or four leading groups, each who take guidance from their statewide leaders. Again, like with the national leadership, state leaders must come from the Resistance rather than a partisan political group. Ideally, leaders should be made up of representatives from various existing smaller groups. This way the smaller working groups can be assured that they have a real and meaningful say in how the state's Resistance works.

Existing smaller groups should not stop what they are doing. The local, community style work they do is largely effective because it is small and local. People like to feel they are part of a community they come to know personally, form relationships with, and with whom they share interests and visions of what society and their local community can be. Thus, while people should still work with their small groups, each state should be able to rally everyone in the Resistance when needed to show a unified force against right-wing extremism. Just as thousands of Indivisible groups tune in to the national organization's weekly agenda and suggestions for actions, current smaller Resistance groups can maintain their small group dynamic while attending to their state's leadership and to the national leadership. Becoming part of a larger movement does not mean one is opting out of participating with their smaller, local groups.

National leaders are not dictators of the movement. It is important to note that leaders do not necessarily articulate the objectives themselves. Nor do they generate all of the ideas for campaigns and actions or contingency plans. Within any large-scale movement, there will be many people who are able to come up with brilliant ideas, and those ideas should be used. Thus, state and national leaders need to elicit input from other Resistance leaders and activists from around the country. It is the job of leaders to coordinate and facilitate smaller actions into larger campaigns. They also need to help smaller actions and campaigns working on local, community issues receive the support and media attention they require.

Training and Education

Training is a vital aspect of successful nonviolent campaigns. Because NVAp involves a wide array of possible tactics and methods, people need to be trained to understand what these are, when to use them, and how to employ them effectively. Furthermore, when faced with a hostile opponent, maintaining nonviolent discipline can be difficult. It is natural for most humans to either run away or violently defend themselves when confronted with angry threats or physical attacks.

When Filipino protestors faced Marcos' military warning them to leave, they remained nonviolent and refused to obey. They risked being pushed, knocked down, dragged away, and even fired upon, but they continued to defy the military's orders in a peaceful manner. Similarly, when African-American civil rights protestors were spit on, verbally abused, and hit with high-pressure hoses, they remained nonviolent, even while police dragged them off. Just as a soldier in a violent war must be taught to face and fight the enemy and not run away, nonviolent protestors who participate in actions where they are likely to meet with hostile opposition will greatly benefit from being taught to not only remain in place but to do so nonviolently. Remaining nonviolent in such situations is not something most people can do; it requires a good deal of practice and training.

In most situations of nonviolent protest, protestors do not need to fear for their physical safety or put themselves in danger of being arrested. This is a major reason why nonviolent action garners a far greater number and diversity of participants than violent conflicts, which is why nonviolent conflicts have a higher success rate than do violent ones.[2] Yet, even in a protest designed and expected to be peaceful, it is important for activists to be aware of how to deal with hostile opposition.

When planning a peaceful and legal action, organizers

should take some basic measures to help the action stays nonviolent. They could remind participants that the best way to deal with anti-protesters is to ignore them. Typically, they are there to provoke Resisters into giving up their moral high ground by becoming violent. Organizers can also refer activists to websites hosted by the ACLU or other similar legal sites that provide Resisters with basic information on what to do if they are approached by police officers. Finally, organizers can make training videos available to activists so they can learn how to remain calm and nonviolent when faced with hostile opponents.

There are many within the movement who are trained in being "peacekeepers," and they are holding workshops to train today's Resisters. For example, some who planned to participate in the 2017 Washington DC Women's March attended training in dealing with pro-Trump protestors. They stood in "hassle lines," a role-playing exercise where half of the participants play the role of peaceful marchers and the other half face them, shouting at them with insults and threats. In other protest demonstrations, marchers learned various methods for staying calm, remaining silent, and walking away.

Organization and leadership, as well as training and education, are all essential to forming and maintaining an effective large-scale nonviolent movement. Like any endeavor involving millions of people, multiple objectives and a complex set of goals, success is far more likely if the movement has been strategically planned. Most resistance movements start out with small groups engaging in ad hoc reactions to what they perceive as an unacceptable policy or practice promulgated by misguided or corrupt rulers. They grow in size and diversity when two things happen: the perceived injustice continues to cause increasing hardship, and the resistance displays itself as honorable in fighting courageously and nonviolently against the injustice. As the Resistance gathers in numbers, it needs educated leaders to organize the campaigns, and it needs trained foot soldiers to help carry out the campaigns.

Overall Goals

Our current Resistance has a broadly construed set of goals. While there is a great deal of disagreement within the Resistance about the direction they wish to see the government take (e.g., some are working towards democratic socialism, others a more extreme left-wing socialist state, and others a more moderate liberal government), Resistance members agree that they want to see Trump and his Congress voted out. They also want to see Trump's impact of right-wing extremists and emboldened hate groups replaced by empowered progressives who protect our democracy, its people, and our natural environment.

There are even some Republicans who oppose Trump because they feel that he and right-wing extremists are ruining the Republican party with their support of white supremacy and an economic policy that will increase rather than decrease the national debt. The goals of the Resistance are broad enough to include moderate Republicans as well as a wide range of liberals and progressives.

An example of an articulated set of goals the Resistance seems to have implicitly adopted are given in the values stated by organizers of the 2018 Cambridge/Boston Women's March.

We are a coalition of diverse social justice, human rights, disability rights, women's rights, and peace organizations that are coming together on the first anniversary of Donald Trump's inauguration ... we seek to ensure the rights of all people to liberty, dignity, and equal protection under the law ... regardless of gender, gender expression, sexual orientation, race, age, religion, nationality, immigration status, disability, economic status, geographical residence, health status, culture, and political affiliation, not just in the United States but across the planet ... and we are committed to protecting and passing laws that protect and sustain the rights of all people ... and the planet itself.[3]

This statement illustrates the direction in which the Resistance is moving. It allows for a wide-range of political viewpoints, from leftist socialists, moderate democrats, and progressive liberals Yet, it is adequately precise in requiring Resistance members to fight for genuine equality and freedom for all. It does not allow for oppression in any form or a disregard for the welfare of our environment.

From these articulated goals, a grand strategy can be developed where various actions are devised as coordinated efforts to achieve these goals. As Gene Sharp described it, a grand strategy "is the overall conception which serves to coordinate and direct all appropriate and available resources ... [of a] group to attain its objectives in a conflict."[4] So, a grand strategy for the Resistance consists of a series of actions, involving a wide range of methods, that work together to achieve various objectives in the overall effort to have our government live up to the values expressed above.

Assessing Strengths and Weaknesses

In any nonviolent movement, it is important to assess the strengths and weaknesses of the resisters and their opposition. This helps resisters effectively strategize a plan that is most likely to be successful. Today's Resistance needs to know what it can rely on (e.g., financial and material resources, human resources, participation levels in various types of actions, public opinion of the movement and its ideology, etc.) and what it needs to keep the movement going forward so it can develop goals, objectives, campaigns, and actions that take these into consideration. Also, by learning where the opposition is vulnerable, the Resistance can target those areas as a way of weakening the opposition. Conversely, by learning where the opposition is strong, the Resistance can work to find ways to counter that strength. Today's Resistance must determine its strengths and the strengths of the Trump regime, as well as the weaknesses of each. Below, I outline each side's strengths, which also indicates the weaknesses of the opposing side.

<u>Trump and Trump-Supporters</u>
1. Trump, right-wing office holders, and wealthy Trump supporters occupy very powerful positions of authority. They have the ability to pass laws and impose sanctions, sometimes quite severe, if those laws are broken.
2. Trump and other elected officials very likely have until November 2018 to do as they see fit with little to no consequences.
3. Koch brothers and other Trumpists are providing the opposition with multi-million-dollar donations to support

their efforts and to fight against any who would oppose them.

4. In mainstream media's efforts to be "fair" and "balanced," they sometimes put a positive spin on what Trump and the GOP are doing, or they at least give Trump and the GOP their side of the story without questioning or criticizing its weaknesses.

5. Fox News and other right-wing media outlets are putting positive spins on all or most that Trump and his supporters are doing, sometimes to the point where they are spreading outright lies, and millions are witnessing this "news" and buying it as truth.

6. The government is dominated by a Republican majority, and nearly all Republicans are choosing Party solidarity over their constituents' wants and needs.

7. The Republicans have successfully rigged our system of voting, and they and their supporters continue to make efforts to rig our voting system so they have a much better chance of winning at the polls than their opponents.

8. Trump and his spokespeople are chipping away at people's confidence in the media, allowing Trump to spread his lies.

9. The Republican majority government has the legal support of the police and military.

10. Trumpism is a rapidly growing and significantly increasing voice in the major decisions that are made at the government level and in the attitudes and behavior of a

growing faction in society.

11. The Resistance, while active and motivated, does not yet have a unified, organized movement, which is needed to more effectively oppose Trump and right-wing extremists.

Resistance

1. Public opinion, as seen by most mainstream media, polls, and visible Resistance protest efforts, are siding with the goals and values of the Resistance.

2. Mueller appears to be gaining ground in his investigations of fraud, obstruction of justice, election interference by Russia, and collusion. This is at least turning public opinion away from Trump and his supporters and in favor of the Resistance. It has also led to indictments of some top government officials, and it may end in arrests for many more.

3. Democrats are winning special elections, flipping seats that were once held by Republicans and where Trump won.

4. Trump, the GOP, and their supporters continue to make themselves look horrific (and thus, by comparison, make the Resistance look good) in the media through actions that would never have been tolerated in any previous administration. Such acts include, but are not limited to: supporting Roy Moore, a man who was fired as a judge and who has been accused by several children of sexual misconduct; refusing to protect the ACA or provide an equal or better alternative to affordable health care; refusing to

take seriously the need to protect our environment from global warming, off-shore drilling, protected parks and land preserves, trophy hunting, just to name a few; turning their backs on the severe suffering of Puerto Ricans; refusing to take measures to stop, and in some instances seeming to outright support, domestic terrorism by white supremacists; and siding with the NRA instead of with the lives and safety of school children and other Americans.

5. Many more Democratic representatives, who were initially relatively complacent, are more actively opposing the GOP because of the Resistance.

6. Mid-term elections are coming up in November 2018, and there is hope that the GOP will be replaced with a Democratic majority.

7. The Resistance is just as motivated, if not more so, as they were over a year ago when Trump was elected. This indicates that the Resistance is dedicated to a long-term fight to defeat not only Trump and the GOP but also the rising voices and power of Trumpism.

8. Information and expertise is available to make the Resistance even more effective as the movement grows and continues to learn how to be better organized and thus more powerful.

What the Resistance Can Do to Build on their Strengths

1. For the Resistance to gain power, they need to make plans that build on their own strengths and further weaken

the opposition by targeting the Trump administration's vulnerabilities. It is important to continue all of the symbolic protests (such as marches, vigils, rallies), and contacting elected officials in order to continue the pressure on those representatives who are or may be willing to stand against Trump.

2. Public opinion must remain with the Resistance, so staying nonviolent and focused on the values such as those espoused by the 2018 Cambridge Women's March will help do this.

3. Commitment to getting Democrats to win in the upcoming special elections as well as the November 2018 mid-term elections is crucial because, although we certainly cannot be assured that the needs and interests of people will be represented by the newly elected representatives, we can be reasonably assured that they will do a far better job than the current right-wing advocates.

4. Finally, getting better organized at both the state and national levels will help the Resistance not only defeat Trump and his cohorts, but it will also empower the people to hold to account newly elected officials and other power holders for meeting the needs of the people rather than their own selfish purposes.

Objectives

Once the values and overall goals are established, the Resistance needs to develop several objectives that will bring them closer to meeting their goals. Objectives are relatively specific, and they must be accompanied by detailed strategic campaigns for achieving them. It is important to note that the purpose here is not to name specific objectives that the Resistance should follow; rather, it is to provide some illustrative examples, so the Resistance can set their own objectives.

Some examples of objectives the Resistance may develop in defeating Trump now and in the future are as follows:

1. Unseat Trump and his supporters in Washington and replace them with people who have a proven record of working to promote Resistance values and goals.
2. Replace the new GOP tax policy with one that supports working class Americans.
3. Pass humane immigration laws that support DREAMERS and allow immigrant families to stay together.
4. Provide affordable high-quality education for all.
5. Investigate the growing problem and seek solutions for addressing white supremacist

terrorism.

6. Rejoin the Paris Climate Agreement and invest in green energy alternatives.

7. Fund Planned Parenthood and other women's health organizations that have lost their funding under this administration.

8. Pass common sense gun legislation.

9. Protect Social Security and Medicare and no longer refer to them as "entitlement" programs.

10. Support labor unions and oppose so-called "right-to-work" laws.

11. Pass a universal health care law or one that similarly provides all Americans with affordable health care.

12. Provide education and training for workers in dying industries.

13. Pass legislation that protects the civil rights of all minority groups.

14. Set up permanent grass-roots, nongovernmental organizations that provide all citizens an equal opportunity to have their voices heard by law makers and who hold representatives to account when they ignore their constituents.

15. Incorporate citizen action training in schools so we develop active, empowered democratic citizens.

Note that each of these are stated in such a way that it would be clear whether they have been achieved or not. Additionally, they each serve as stepping-stones to reaching the overall goals of the Resistance.

Although new horrors occur almost weekly, and sometimes even daily, in our government's attacks against vulnerable populations and the environment, the Resistance needs to prioritize their objectives. However, there is no reason to take on only one objective at a time. The Resistance is large and diverse enough, and if it becomes organized, it could work toward several objectives simultaneously. While a coalition of environmental groups can engage in efforts to protect our planet, women's and other minority rights groups can work to meet objectives that promote the rights and freedoms of women and other oppressed groups. Gun safety resistors can unite to fight for reasonable gun legislation, economic justice advocates can participate in actions that support economic equality, and so on.

There will be some actions that will require all factions of the Resistance to come together as one, such as making our schools safer against gun violence, protecting Mueller's investigation, protecting immigrant families, and calling for Trump's impeachment. However, different interest groups can take on separate issues while maintaining a massive impact on the opposition. Depending on the objective, then, leaders can help plan an action that calls on particular interest groups or the entire Resistance.

Even with established priorities, however, the Resistance must be flexible to allow it to respond to a new crisis or emergency. While stricter gun legislation was always an important concern for the Resistance, it wasn't until the Parkland, Florida shooting that it became a predominant issue in most American's minds. Students, parents, educators and citizens from across the country, from far-left to conservative political ideologies united in their intolerance of Congress refusing to enact sensible gun laws. Similarly, though immigrant rights have been a consistent concern of Resisters, when Trump's Zero-Tolerance policy went into effect and ICE agents took children away from their parents with no information or plan to reunite them in the future, the nation united in protest against this cruelly inhumane policy. When such events occur that rally the majority of Americans, the Resistance must be willing and able to switch priorities and act in accordance with the newly energized populace. Other objectives are not dropped. Rather, they must be reprioritized.

Campaigns

Campaigns are a set of actions designed to reach a given objective. For example, The Montgomery Bus Boycott was a campaign with the objective of ending segregation on public transportation in Alabama. This objective was part of a broader goal of overturning so called "separate but equal" policies in public spaces. The boycott was made up of several different actions and methods including civil disobedience by Rosa Parks in refusing to give up her seat to a white patron; a general boycott, which consisted of masses of people, primarily African-Americans, refusing to take the buses; providing affordable alternatives to riding the buses, including reduced cab fares; marches and rallies to speak out against segregation; letters to the editor and public speeches explaining the offensiveness and oppressive nature of segregation; and negotiations with city officials. The campaign, then, was what became known as the Bus Boycott and it involved a variety of different nonviolent strategically organized actions that took place over the period of approximately one year.

In today's Resistance, perhaps the best example of a campaign occurred after the Parkland, Florida school shooting on February 14, 2018. Although it was not planned out as a campaign, it has many features of one. The stated objective was to enact sensible gun laws. This objective is not overly specific, which allows it to bring together people from different perspectives on the issue of gun violence. Some may want Congress to pass legislation banning assault weapons similar to the ban enacted by Congress in 1994, which banned not only the purchase, sale, and manufacturing of the weapons but also large capacity ammunition feeding devices. Others simply want better enforcement of background checks, and others are willing to accept any movement, regardless of how small, toward passing legislation that will reduce gun violence in our schools and across the country.

Several actions employing different methods were planned and enacted over a period of time to achieve a specific objective. The campaign started out with a call to action from survivors of the shooting. They called for people to gather together on March 24, 2018 in D.C. and in cities around the country to March for Our Lives. In addition, two other events went viral on social media. One called "Enough!" was a 17-minute student, teacher, and administrator walk out at 10:00 a.m. on March 14 to commemorate the 17 children who lost their lives in Parkland. Another walkout was also planned for a month later on April 20 (the anniversary of the Columbine shooting) where students, educators, and community members gathered on school grounds to call for gun reform. Other actions also took place after the shooting such as a student "die in" outside the White House on Feb 19.

Sketching out some ideas of different actions, including methods from the different categories outlined in Chapter Four, may have helped maintain this level of energy long enough to force the implementation of changes. For example, more symbolic methods could have been planned such as marches and rallies. Also, more political involvement methods could have been organized, such as flooding legislators' phone lines at certain times every week to pressure them to pass sensible gun laws. Teachers could have engaged in methods of disruption and coercion by engaging in a massive work-to-rule action, or parents could have decided to keep their children home and homeschool them until sensible gun laws are passed. While some of these methods were discussed on social media, nothing was definitively planned or enacted. If planned out carefully, methods of disobedience could have been developed such as massive student sick-outs, or if colleges agreed to not punish students for any reprisals they may suffer from their schools, students could have engaged in a national walk-out for one day every week until laws were changed.

As with any complex endeavor, planning significantly increases the likelihood that the desired goals will be achieved. No one would expect any sort of success to come from an unplanned war with untrained soldiers and uneducated leaders. Because NVAp requires a similar amount of organization and planning as war, it is essential that the Resistance form a culturally diverse national leadership. It is also important that they develop a strategically planned movement with overall goals and objectives. Training and education should also be made widely available so Resisters learn to remain nonviolent, even in the face of hostile opposition, and so they learn to develop hundreds of different methods, each designed to take on a particular issue or set of issues based on their analysis of the strengths and weaknesses of the opposition.

Because Trump is the extreme example of a much larger problem with American government and American society, defeating him is only a partial solution. The Resistance would greatly benefit from employing NVAp to develop long-term strategies that target not only Trump but also Trumpism, the growing, dangerous movement to more firmly entrench oppressive practices and policies that are harming our most vulnerable populations. Additionally, this movement is gaining ground world-wide; thus, the Resistance against it in the US is a critical part of opposing it as a global trend.

Chapter Six
Shifting the Balance of Power

This chapter builds on the previous one by using the information from the beginning of the book and applying it to today's Resistance. By looking at how the Resistance can target and topple the pillars of support upon which Trump and his supporters stand, today's Resisters can learn how to become even more successful in removing Trump and right-wing extremists. This is an essential first step in moving our country toward a more inclusive, diverse, and empowered democracy.

After Trump, our country cannot afford to sit idly by and trust that our new leaders will act in our best interests. Instead, we need an empowered people who will act in an organized and effective manner to ensure that all political leaders will truly represent their constituents instead of private and big-money interests. I look at how the Resistance can become the impetus for developing more permanent democratic structures where the people form relationships, grassroots organizations, and a means of mobilizing to engage in actions that will have a significant and meaningful impact on our elected officials and the escalating power of Trumpism. We need to protect our democracy from the corruption that arises when the vast majority of power is left unchecked in the hands of a few. We must create people-powered decisional structures in society that help make our government by, of, and for the people.

Pillars of Support

As discussed in chapter three on Understanding Power, the pillars of support are what enable Trump, the GOP, and their associates to have power. For the Resistance to formulate objectives and develop campaigns that can effectively take Trump and his supporters down, it is important to target these pillars. Below, I look at each of them and offer suggestions on how each can be toppled so Trump and his supporters fall off. We need to make room for better people to take their place in a system more accountable to the people.

Public Service

Anytime a resistance group plans an action, they must be mindful of the impact it will have on the general public. If a workers' strike, for example, endangers the public welfare, it will have a larger negative impact on the public than on

151

the rulers. This is why it is rarely a good idea for health care employees or firefighters to strike. The same can be said of public transportation workers. Although people's lives are not at stake, their livelihoods may very well be if they cannot get to work. Teachers striking can also cause undue hardship on children and families. Yet, even these events can be effective if they represent the will of the people opposing a harsh and even at times cruel set of leaders, as Trump and his cohorts are proving to be.

There are alternative ways of shifting the allegiance of public servants to the people and away from corrupt leaders. Teachers, for example, can work-to-rule rather than strike. Transportation workers can strike for a day every month instead of for days at a time. We have seen some cases of public servants refusing to comply with Trump's demands. Police in many towns and cities around the country refused to act as agents of ICE, many public officials established sanctuary cities to protect DREAMERS, and some city officials are marching with students protesting gun violence. There are ways, then, for public service employees to show they both stand with the people and will not unquestionably follow the dictates of the power holders. The Resistance should continue to foster relationships with public servants and support them when they engage in even relatively small resistance actions.

Military

Obviously, the military is still very much under the authority of the government. Yet, there has been some resistance moves on their part. Top ranking military personnel expressed surprise when Trump stated he wanted to repeal Obama's ban on enlisting transgender troops, and they were reluctant to carry out Trump's wishes. Fortunately, four federal judges overruled Trump in December 2017.[1] The military also showed a willingness to separate themselves from Trump with their disapproval of Trump's request for a military parade. According to The Hill, "Eighty-nine percent of Military Times readers responded with, 'No, it's a waste of money and troops are too busy."[2]

The Resistance should respect the importance of our military giving due deference to their Commander-in-Chief. However, given Trump's instability and unreliability, the Resistance should also support the military's efforts to question such things as a military parade, which seems only to serve the needs of Trumps' ego rather than the good of our country. Having the Pentagon postpone the parade to an indefinite date is a sign that the military is already questioning Trump's agenda. The Resistance should also push sympathetic elected officials to support Senator Markey and Representative Lieu's proposed legislation to prevent the President from being able to call on the military to launch a first nuclear strike without prior approval from Congress.[3]

Political Party

If right-wing extremists begin to lose the support of other Republicans, they will not be able to pass legislation, and they will have a very difficult time raising donations for their re-election. A few Republicans *have* spoken out against Trump, such as Senator Jeff Flake, and others such as the 20 Republicans who voted against repealing the ACA on May 2017. They have shown that they will sometimes refuse to support the Party's legislative efforts. The Resistance needs to keep putting pressure on Republicans to choose their constituents over their Party by keeping up with phone calls to law makers and showing up at legislative hearings. They can also applaud in social media any Republican voters who speak out against Trump's policies to show that the Resistance is not politically partisan but a friend to all who support the goals of democracy, equity, safety, and environmental health.

Getting members of a political party to side against their own Party is difficult, but it is possible. It is not likely that committed Trump fans will budge. But there are plenty of Republicans who can be persuaded to vote against their party if Trump and his destructive policies continue to go unchecked. This is best achieved by remaining nonviolent and nonpartisan. While it is okay to support candidates from a particular party because they offer to resolve the disputed policies, the Resistance must be clear that it will oppose any candidate, regardless of political party, if they do not support their wishes, and conversely, they will advocate for any candidate who supports their wishes.

Labor Organizations

One of the best ways to weaken the power of Trump is to engage in nationwide workers' strikes. This takes national organization to be effective; thus, the Resistance will need to get more organized. A way to employ strikes without disrupting people's lives too much or endangering workers' ability to get paid is to alternate from one labor organization to another. So, steelworkers may strike one day, machinists another, foodservice people another, and so on. One of the most powerful impacts of nationwide strikes is they show the government that the Resistance is very organized on a massive scale. Alternating single day strikes, therefore, would illustrate that the people have the ability and willingness to engage in a unified campaign to undermine the authority of the government; it would indicate that the Resistance has the loyalty and cooperation of the people far more than does the government.

Public Opinion

To sway public opinion away from the opposition, the Resistance needs to continue what they are doing by staying nonviolent. They need to publish their pursuit of political, social, and economic equity, human rights for all, protection of the environment, safeguarding vulnerable populations, and protecting fundamental rights and freedoms of our democracy. They can also go further by attacking the media that is promoting the ideas, actions, and agenda of the right-wing extremists. Fox News' primetime news shows have virtually become State-sponsored television, often going to absurd lengths to put a positive spin on Trump's policy proposals, his actions, and his comments. They more than any other media outlet are legitimizing and promoting Trump and the dangerous domestic terrorism he inspires.

Building on the effective efforts of boycotting Hannity's sponsors when he backed Roy Moore, organizing a nationwide boycott of Fox News' major sponsors, then possibly moving on to boycott all of their sponsors, will likely either get them to cancel their programs or, more probably, change them so they are far less biased. The same could be done against Rush Limbaugh, Alex Jones, and Breitbart once the Fox News campaign succeeds. If it does succeed, other programs will have reason to be very concerned about the ability of the Resistance to shut them down or force them to change.

A final and very important way to earn public trust and respect is to achieve success. If people continue march and make calls to legislators but don't see significant changes, they may start to lose interest in the Resistance. To achieve more success, the Resistance must get nationally organized and start engaging in disruptive and noncompliant methods that force change, methods that target the pillars of support upon which our rulers rely.

Allies

Trump has fired numerous aides he once considered important allies because they did something he saw as a threat to him. One of his closest aides, Director of Strategic Communications Hope Hicks, resigned after being criticized by Trump for speaking to special council Mueller regarding the Trump-Russia investigation. Even with his own son-in-law, Trump refused to speak in defense of Jared Kushner maintaining his top-level security clearance. If a leader seems very fearful that he will be betrayed, convincing him that his associates are not loyal is a good way to isolate him from those on whom he most relies.

The Resistance will not likely be successful in converting Trumpists to reject the hate they have so eagerly embraced and are becoming more empowered to display in public. It may be best, then, for Resisters to focus on everyone else who is open to embracing the values, attitudes, practices, and policies of inclusion, support, and sustainability. These can be promoted through symbolic methods of nonviolence that illustrate the harm Trump causes. If the Resistance can highlight the hateful actions of Trump, we may not convert loyal Trump supporters but we can, in time, force those attitudes back into the shadows. In time, we may even convince some of his supporters to be more compassionate and open, at least some of them and to some degree.

By targeting these pillars of support, the Resistance needs to get organized and outline objectives that go after these pillars. They need to devise campaigns and actions that help them reach the objectives they set. Finally, they should strategize plans that target Trump's weaknesses so the pillars that hold up him and his supporters will be shifted to empower the people and more progressive representatives.

Our government is supposed to work for us, the people. And as we have seen, its power is entirely dependent on the people's willingness to cooperate in the areas described. For the Resistance to redistribute the balance of power, they need to engage in strategic withdrawal of their obedience so that power transfers away from Trump as well as corrupt governors in general, and into the hands of more representative leaders and the people. Methods of noncompliance and disobedience require that the Resistance looks at the three reasons people obey, each of which are discussed theoretically in Chapter Three and re-examined below more practically in terms of today's Resistance.

Willingness to Obey

<u>Legitimacy of Rulers</u>
Trump was elected with questionable legitimacy because, although he won the Electoral College, he lost by over three million votes in the popular vote. Furthermore, his selection of top advisors and cabinet members branded him as a racist, misogynist, and Wall Street supporter, providing proof that the promises he made during his campaign were a lie: he is not black and brown people's best chance, he does not love women more than anyone else, and he is not "draining the swamp." His legitimacy continued to spiral downward by his repeated failure to pass legislation, including his immigration ban, repeal and replace or even just repeal the Affordable Care Act (ACA), and funding for a border wall between the US and Mexico. Finally, as members of the Trump administration resign, and as the head of Special Counsel investigation on Russian interference continues to find more evidence of Trump's corruption his legitimacy sinks lower to a point where, according to media polls, the majority of Americans think he should be impeached.

In addition to Trump, the right-wing GOP is also losing legitimacy. While they initially represented the possible sane voices to check Trump's absurd claims and proposals, they have repeatedly shown themselves to support Trump in virtually everything he seeks to do. Additionally, they are supporting legislation of their own that violates the interests of their constituents: from threatening net neutrality, passing a tax bill that benefits only the wealthy at the serious detriment to the working classes, attacking women's reproductive rights, supporting a repeal of the Dodd-Frank regulations, and refusing to pass common sense gun legislation. Perhaps most troubling of all, the GOP seem to be turning a blind eye to Trump's inexplicably close and friendly relationship with Russian leader Putin, and to the mounting evidence of Trump's obstruction of justice, financial fraud, and collusion with Russia during his election.

Making sure such acts are publicized in the news and on social media and explaining how such claims of corruption are supported by ample evidence is helping to delegitimize Trump and the GOP in the eyes of a growing number of people. This is helping the Resistance to grow, and it's inspiring some within the Resistance to start taking direct action against the White House and the Republican leaders by engaging in disruptive methods, such as boycotts, and in acts of civil disobedience, such as student walkouts and occupying government offices.

Ability to Impose Sanctions

As of yet, we do not have a dictatorship. Thus, our government is not able to impose the sort of harsh reprisals of such authoritarian regimes as Duterte's, Putin's, Erdogen's, or Kim Jun Un's. Yet, we do see today's government leaders imposing sanctions that are more typical in a democracy. We see right-wing conservatives claim that protesting against Trump's policies is anti-American, and approximately 20 states are seeking to impose further limitations to legal protest.[4] We also see fiscal conservatives try convincing the populace that cutting taxes for the wealthy stimulates the economy by creating jobs for working class people. Trump and his racist allies attempt to silence protest by labeling Kaepernick and his supporters as anti-American for taking a knee. Thus, both sanctions and manipulating people's beliefs about the benefits of compliance have an impact on whether people obey their governors or join the Resistance.

More and more, people are not identifying patriotism as blindly complying with Trump and his hateful supporters. Instead, many are seeing their resistance to these leaders as patriotic because it is a defense of our much-cherished democratic principles. Furthermore, many see that today's government is not acting in the best interests of the people. A growing number of people are coming to believe that resisting powerful Trumpists in society and the media as well as those in government is a far more virtuous path than following along with policies that harm the environment and put at risk marginalized people.

Strength and Integrity of the Resistance Movement
The Resistance movement started out with record-breaking

protests across the country and in major cities around the world with the Women's March. Other massive marches followed: the Science and Climate marches, which protested the anti-science approach of the Trump administration in their climate change denial; the flash protests at major airports around the country opposing Trump's immigration ban; and the massive student marches protesting inadequate gun legislation. Political involvement methods also continue. Many of them are organized by Indivisible and other local Resistance groups who put continual and significant pressure on local, state, and federal elected officials to oppose the Trump agenda.

There are several reasons the Resistance has continued to gain credibility. First, their promotion of equity and justice for all cultural groups has given them the moral high ground. Also, their commitment to legal and nonviolent methods of opposition and protest have earned them respect. It helps that they oppose the racist, misogynistic, homophobic, transphobic, and economic elitism of Trump and his cohorts. Their success in getting elected representatives to speak out against the Trump agenda is giving them more legitimacy as are the impressive wins for Democrats in special local elections in Republican dominated voting districts.

Maintaining credibility is crucial for the Resistance to win converts away from the shrinking number of Trump supporters whom he needs to claim legitimacy of rule. By addressing the three reasons people tend to give their allegiance and cooperation to rulers, the Resistance can generate enough support to engage in strategic methods of disruption and noncompliance. These are essential if the Resistance is to shift power away from Trump and into the hands of a more accountable and representative group of elected officials.

After Trump

Once Trump is gone, the Resistance can move from opposing Trump to fighting the dangerous impact he has inspired. Additionally, it can focus more on building and promoting democratic participatory structures rather than almost exclusively on resisting. The Resistance can become a people's movement that works with the organizations, relationships, and structures it has built to create systemic changes in the decision-making processes in our society. To effectively counter the long-term damage of Trump, the Resistance can help sustain and further the knowledge many people have acquired about their local, state, and national government, how it works and how it may need to change. Furthermore, they can make permanent the organizations they formed through the Resistance in order to continue to speak and act out against oppressive and harmful practices and policies of corporations, Trumpist groups, and anti-labor organizations.

A democracy involves far more than voting. By bolstering the energy and momentum inspired by the first efforts to oppose Trump, we the people can reclaim our power. We can truly defeat the hateful impact Trump has engendered domestically and, in turn, help reverse its increasing strength throughout the world.

Nonviolent action has a very long history, from the present day going back to the successful plebeian movement in 4th century BCE to gain a voice in the Patrician government.[5] At its most basic level, nonviolent action works to undermine the authority of rulers by showing them, through a series of resistance campaigns, that their power is entirely dependent on the willing cooperation of the people. In democracies, citizens have the opportunity to replace government leaders by voting them out and voting in others to take their place. The belief is that the right to vote gives people a ruling influence over their representatives. As we see, however, this too often does not turn out to be the case. Instead, Americans are more and more experiencing a government who has lost touch with its people, and thereby enacting policies and laws that best serve the interests of the wealthy who can afford to finance their election campaigns and lobbying efforts.

It is inevitable that people will have differing views on politics, and therefore we cannot expect that all will agree with the policies of their elected officials. Yet, when our government representatives are so distant from their constituents that they are unwilling to listen, to understand, or to attend to their needs, then one option is to replace them with others who will be more attentive. When, however, our government has established habits and systems where they are far more influenced by money than the needs of the people, voting in new leaders may not do enough to have a truly representative government. Thus, nonviolent action does more than get people to vote; it helps citizens counter the long-term impacts of corrupt rulers by instituting permanent decision-making structures that empower the people.

To defeat Trump now and the impact he will have in our future, both in and outside government, the Resistance must continue doing what it is doing. Furthermore, it must grow stronger by becoming more organized, so it may successfully achieve its clearly articulated goals. By following the theories of NVAp and following the guidance of Resistance leaders in enacting nonviolent campaigns, today's Resistance can be a united force that shifts the balance of power away from Trump and his emboldened supporters and into the hands of newly elected government, corporate, and societal leaders. It can form a system that holds elected officials far more accountable to the people. In short, by adopting the organization, structure, and techniques advocated by NVAp, the Resistance can safeguard human rights as well as the environment and help strengthen our democratic society for a more peaceful, free, and equitable way of living.

References

Introduction

1. See, for example, works by Gene Sharp, Erica Chenoweth, Kurt Schock, Sharon Erikson Nepstad, and Timothy Ash.

2. Polychronious, C.J. "The Anatomy of Trumpocracy: An Interview with Noam Chomsky." June 28, 2018. https://truthout.org/articles/the-anatomy-of-trumpocracy-an-interview-with-noam-chomsky/

3. Filipovic, Jill. CNN. "Presidential seal on Trump golf tees? A new low." 3:47 PM ET, Tue March 6, 2018. https://www.cnn.com/2018/03/06/opinions/trump-presidential-seal-for-golf-tee-filipovic/index.html

4. Zanona, Melanie. "Trump cuts funds to fight anti-right wing violence." 6:35 PM EDT, August 14, 2017. http://thehill.com/policy/national-security/346552-trump-cut-funds-to-fight-anti-right-wing-violence

Chapter One

1. R.A. The Economist. The Economist Explains Thomas Piketty's "Capital," summarized in four paragraphs: A very brief summary of 'Capital' in the Twenty-first Century." May 5, 2015. https://www.economist.com/blogs/economist-explains/2014/05/economist-explains

2. Palast, Greg. "The Best Democracy Money Can Buy." Documentary. October 19, 2016

3. Bui, Quoctrung and Nate Cohn. NYTimes. "Adventures in Extreme Gerrymandering: See the Fair and Wildly Unfair Maps We Made for Pennsylvania." Jan 17, 2018.
www.nytimes.com/interactive/2018/01/17/upshot/pennsylvania-gerrymandering.html

4. De Vogue, Ariane. CNN. "Supreme Court grants North Carolina Republicans partial victory in gerrymander case." 7:41 PM ET, Tue February 6, 2018.
https://www.cnn.com/2018/02/06/politics/north-carolina-gerrymandering/index.html

5. Carriat, Julie and Michaela Cabrera. Reuters. "HRW says Trump is 'disaster' for human rights, fuels authoritarians. Jan 18, 2018 10:11 AM.
https://ca.reuters.com/article/topNews/idCAKBN1F7210-OCATP

6. Hernandez, Salvador. BuzzFeed News. "The US Should Have a 'President For Life' Like China." March 3, 2018 10:05 PM.
https://www.buzzfeed.com/salvadorhernandez/president-trump-joked-that-maybe-the-us-should-have-a?utm_term=.gbEzmwlRY#.maJNjyJgA

7. Rucker, Philip. The Washing Post. "Trump praises Kim's authoritarian rule, says 'I want my people to do the same.'" June 15, 2018 10:44 AM.
https://www.washingtonpost.com/politics/trump-praises-kims-authoritarian-rule-says-i-want-my-people-to-do-the-

same/2018/06/15/cea20aa2-70a5-11e8-bf86-
a2351b5ece99_story.html?utm_term=.151dd1a953c0&tid
=sm_fb

8.   Aiello, Chloe. CNBC. "Donor threatens to withhold
GOP campaign contributions unless the party takes a stand
against guns." 5:41 PM ET Sat, 17 Feb 2018.
https://www.cnbc.com/2018/02/17/gop-donor-issues-an-
ultimatum-on-guns-nytimes.html

9.   Konnikova, Maria. Politico Magazine. "Trump's Lies
vs. Your Brain." January/February 2017.
https://www.politico.com/magazine/story/2017/01/donal
d-trump-lies-liar-effect-brain-214658

10. Kertscher, Tom. PolitiFact. "Were the 7 nations
identified in Donald Trump's travel ban named by Barack
Obama as terror hotbeds?" Tuesday, February 7th, 2017
5:00 AM.
http://www.politifact.com/wisconsin/statements/2017/fe
b/07/reince-priebus/were-7-nations-identified-donald-
trumps-travel-ban/

11.   Hirschfeld, Davis and Somini Sengupta. The New
York Times. "Trump Administration Rejects Study Showing
Positive   Impact   of   Refugees."   Sept   18,   2017.
https://www.nytimes.com/2017/09/18/us/politics/refuge
es-revenue-cost-report-trump.html

12. ACLU. "End the Use of Religion to Discriminate."
2018. https://www.aclu.org/issues/religious-liberty/using-
religion-discriminate/end-use-religion-discriminate

13. Cohen, Claire. The Telegraph. "Donald Trump sexism tracker: Every offensive comment in one place." 14 July 2017 9:03 AM.

https://www.telegraph.co.uk/women/politics/donald-trump-sexism-tracker-every-offensive-comment-in-one-place/

14. Trump, Donald. Twitter 7:58AM – June 29, 2017 @realDonaldTrump

15. Trump, Donald. Twitter 8:03AM – Dec 12, 2017 @realDonaldTrump

16. Gottbrath, Laurin-Whitney. Aljazeera. "One year under Trump: 'An assault on women's health.'" 21 Jan 2018. https://www.aljazeera.com/news/2018/01/year-trump-assault-womens-health-180121144023315.html

17. Mooney, Chris, Brady Dennis, and Steven Mufson. Washington Post. "Trump names Scott Pruitt, Oklahoma attorney general suing EPA on climate change, to head the EPA. December 8, 2016.

https://www.washingtonpost.com/news/energy-environment/wp/2016/12/07/trump-names-scott-pruitt-oklahoma-attorney-general-suing-epa-on-climate-change-to-head-the-epa/?utm_term=.a210fe5b81c5

18. Greshko, Michael, Laura Parker, and Brian Clark Howard. National Geographic. "A Running List of How Trump Is Changing the Environment." March 23, 2018. https://news.nationalgeographic.com/2017/03/how-trump-is-changing-science-environment/

19. Merica, Dan. CNN. "Nearly every governor with ocean coastline opposes Trump's drilling proposal." 2:20 PM ET Fri January 12, 2018.
 https://www.cnn.com/2018/01/11/politics/governors-ocean-coastline-offshore-drilling-trump/index.html

20. Eckhouse, Brian, Ari Natter, and Chris Martin. Bloomberg. "Trump's Tarrifs on Solar Mark Biggest Blow to Renewbles Yet." January 23, 2018 4:38:54 AM EST. https://www.bloomberg.com/news/articles/2018-01-22/trump-taxes-solar-imports-in-biggest-blow-to-clean-energy-yet

21. Carrington, Damian. The Guardian. "Earth's sixth mass extinction even under say, scientists warn." Mon 10 Jul 2017 15.00 EDT.
https://www.theguardian.com/environment/2017/jul/10/earths-sixth-mass-extinction-event-already-underway-scientists-warn

22. http://www.ushistory.org/Declaration/document/

23. Dewey, John. Democracy and Education. Simon and Brown, simonandbrown.com. 2012, p. 50.

24. Locke, John. Two Treatises of Government. (Mark Goldie, ed.). Everyman, London. 1924/1993.

25. Rawls, John. A Theory of Justice. Belknap Press. Cambridge, MA. 1971

Chapter Two

1.   Lackey, Douglas P. The Ethics of War and Peace.

Pearson. London, UK. 1989.

2.   Schock, Kurt. Civil Resistance Today. Polity Press. Cambridge UK. 2015.

3.   Vinthagen, Stellan. A Theory of Nonviolent Action: How Civil Resistance Works. Zed Books, Ltd. London, UK. 2015.

4.   Brock-Utne, Birgit. Educating for Peace: A Feminist Perspective. Pergamon Press. NY. 1985, p. 74.

5.   Young, Iris Marion. Justice and the Politics of Difference. Princeton University Press. Princeton, NJ. 1990, p. 39.

6.   Herb, G. H. The geography of peace movements. In C. Flint (Ed.), The geography of war and peace: From death camps to diplomats (pp. 347-368). Oxford: Oxford University Press. 2005.

7.   Gandhi, M. K. The Gandhi reader: A sourcebook of his life and writings. H. A. Jack (Ed.). New York, NY: Grove Press. 1956.

8.   Walton, M. A woman's crusade: Alice Paul and the battle for the ballot. New York, NY: Palgrave Macmillan. 2010.

9.   Anderson, T. H. The movement and the sixties: Protest in America from Greensboro to Wounded Knee. New York, NY: Oxford University Press. 1995.

10.   Gandhi, M. K. The Gandhi reader: A sourcebook of his life and writings. H. A. Jack (Ed.). New York, NY: Grove Press. 1956.

11. Ibid.

12. Gandhi, M.K. Nonviolent Resistance (Satyagraha). Dover Publications, Inc., Mineola. 2001, p. 77.

13. Atak, Iain Nonviolence in Political Theory. Edinburgh University Press, Edinburgh, UK. 2012.

14. Gandhi, M.K. Nonviolent Resistance (Satyagraha). Dover Publications, Inc., Mineola. 2001, p. 43.

15. Ibid., 67.

16. Chenoweth, Erica and Maria J. Stephan. Why Civil Resistance Works: The Strategic Logic of Nonviolent Conflict. Columbia University Press. New York, NY. 2011.

17. Sharp, Gene. Social Power and Political Freedom. Porter Sargent Publishers, Inc., Boston, MA. 1980.

18. Weber, Thomas. Nonviolence is Who? Gene Sharp and Gandhi. Peace & Change. 28, no.. 2 (2003): 257.

19. Taylor, Matthew. The Guardian. "'White Europe': 60,000 nationalists march on Poland's independence day." Sun 12 Nov 2017 11.36 EST. https://www.theguardian.com/world/2017/nov/12/white-europe-60000-nationalists-march-on-polands-independence-day

20. Howe, Kenneth R. Understanding Equal Educational Opportunity: Social Justice, Democracy, and Schooling. Teachers College Press. New York, NY. 1997.

21. Ibid.

22. Ibid., 27-28.

23. Ibid., 39.

24. Ibid., 32.

25. Langford, Tom. "Union Democracy as a Foundation for a Participatory Society: A Theoretical Elaboration and Historical Example." Labour/Le Travail. 76, Fall 2015: 79-108.

26. Ibid.

27. Corbett, Steven. "A Critical Qualitative Study of the Relationship between Social Empowerment and Participatory Democracy in the UK." International Journal of Social Quality. 4 (1), Summer 2014: 7-25.

Chapter Three

1. Chomsky, Noam. Hegemony or Survival. 2003, pp. 7-8.

2. Arendt, Hannah. On Revolution. Penguin Classics – need full citation

3. Tolstoy, Leo. The Kingdom of God is Within You. Translated by Constance Garnett. Kshetra Books, 2016/1894.

4. Gandhi, Nonviolent Resistance p. 15

5. Sharp, Social Power and Political Freedom

6. Roberts, Adam and Timothy Ash. Civil Resistance & Power Politics: The Experience of Non-violent Action from Gandhi to the Present. Oxford University Press. Oxford, UK. 2011, p. 301-302.

7. Makalintal, Joshua. Waging Nonviolence. "The challenges of building a united resistance in Duterte's

Philippines." March 14, 2018.
https://wagingnonviolence.org/feature/united-resistance-duterte-philippines/

8. Nepstad, Sharon Erikson. Nonviolent Struggles: Theories, Strategies, & Dynamics. Oxford University Press. New York, NY. 2015.

9. Sharp, Gene. There Are Realistic Alternatives. Cambridge: The Albert Einstein Institution, 2003.

10. Sharp, Gene. From Dictatorship to Democracy.

11. Ibid.

12. Sharp, Gene. The Politics of Nonviolent Action: Part Two. The Methods of Nonviolent Action. Boston: Porter Sargent Publishers, 1973.

13. Ibid.

14. Nepstad. Nonviolent Struggles.

Chapter Four

1. Sharp. The Politics of Nonviolent Action: Part Two.

2. Ibid., 117.

3. Ibid., 183.

4. Ibid.

5. Ibid.

6. Nepstad. Nonviolent Struggles.

7. Gates, Henry Louis, Jr. Colored People: A Memoir. 1994

8. Sharp, The Politics of Nonviolent Action: Part Two.

9. Suhl, Yuri. They Fought Back: The Story of the

Jewish Resistance in Nazi Europe. 1967.

10. Moore, Michael. The Awful Truth. "HMO Funeral." Season 1, Episode 1. DVD.

11. Atwood, Margaret. The Handmaid's Tale. Anchor Books. anchorbooks.com 1998.

12. Littell, R. The Czech Black Book. 1969.

13. Durando, Jessica. USA Today. "March for Our Lives could be the biggest single-day protest in D.C.'s history. 3:57 PM EDT Mar 25, 2018.
https://www.usatoday.com/story/news/nation/2018/03/24/march-our-lives-could-become-biggest-single-day-protest-d-c-nations-history/455675002/

14. Chenoweth, Erica and Maria J. Stephan. Why Civil Resistance Works. p. 10.

15. Roberts, Adam and Timothy Ash. Civil Resistance & Power Politics.

16. Arrow, Ruaridh. How to Start a Revolution. Documentary. DVD. Feb 24, 2012.

17. Indivisible Website.
https://www.indivisible.org/about-us/

18. Pengelly, Martin. The Guardian. "Democrat Doug Jones: Trump shouldn't resign over sexual misconduct claims." Sunday 17 Dec 2017 10.13 EST.
https://www.theguardian.com/us-news/2017/dec/17/doug-jones-democrat-roy-moore-donald-trump

19. Williams, Juan. Eyes on the Prize: American's Civil

Rights Years 1954-1965. Penguin Books. New York, NY. 1987

20. Ibid.

21. Sharp. The Politics of Nonviolent Action: Part Two, p. 223.

22. Roberts, Adam and Timothy Ash. Civil Resistance & Power Politics.

23. Gittleson, Kim. BBC News. "Market Basket: Workers risk it all for their boss." 1 August 2014.
http://www.bbc.com/news/business-28580359

24. Shock, Kurt. Unarmed Insurrections: People Power Movements in Nondemocracies. University of Minnesota Press. Minneapolis MN. 2005.

25. Sharp. The Politics of Nonviolent Action: Part Two.

26. Aiello, Chloe. CNBC. "Donor threatens to withhold GOP campaign contributions unless the party takes a stand against guns." 7:11 AM ET Tue, 20 Feb 2018. https://www.cnbc.com/2018/02/17/gop-donor-issues-an-ultimatum-on-guns-nytimes.html

27. Sharp, Gene. From Dictatorship to Democracy: A Conceptual Framework for Liberation. The Albert Einstein Institute. Cambridge, MA. 1993.

28. Sharp, Gene. The Politics of Nonviolent Action: Part Three. The Dynamics of Nonviolent Action. Boston: Porter Sargent Publishers, 1973, p. 743.

Chapter Five

1. Sharp. The Politics of Nonviolent Action: Part Two,

p. 18.

2.   Chenoweth, Erica and Maria J. Stephan. Why Civil Resistance Works.

3.   Cambridge/Boston Women's March. https://en-us.fievent.com/

4.   Sharp. There Are Realistic Alternatives, p. 20.

Chapter Six

1.   Savage, David G. LA Times. "Military poised to accept transgender troops, despite Trump tweets, as courts block ban." Dec 26, 2017. 2:20 PM.
http://www.latimes.com/politics/la-na-pol-transgender-military-20171226-story.html

2.   Carter, Brandon. The Hill. "Military Times poll: Majority oppose Trump's military parade." Feb 08, 2018. 8:23 PM EST. http://thehill.com/blogs/blog-briefing-room/news/373072-military-times-poll-majority-oppose-trumps-military-parade

3.   Link, Taylor. Salon. "Democrats propose legislation to prevent Donald Trump from launching a nuclear first strike." Jan 25, 2017. 6:00 PM.
https://www.salon.com/2017/01/25/democrats-propose-legislation-that-prevent-donald-trump-from-launching-a-nuclear-first-strike/

4.   Greensblatt, Alan. Governing. "As Protests Escalate Under Trump, States Seek New Ways to Deter Them." Sept 20, 2017. http://www.governing.com/topics/politics/gov-

protests-st-louis-states-laws-restrictions.html

5.   Sharp. The Politics of Nonviolent Action: Part Two.

CPSIA information can be obtained
at www.ICGtesting.com
Printed in the USA
FFHW02n0839180918
48407524-52264FF